HEINEMAN BOOKSHELF

Ballads

Wordsworth & Coleridge

Edited by Carole Coates

Series Editor: Andrew Whittle
Series Consultant: Virginia Graham

Heinemann Educational,
a division of Heinemann Publishers (Oxford) Ltd
Halley Court, Jordan Hill, Oxford OX2 8EJ

OXFORD LONDON EDINBURGH
MADRID ATHENS BOLOGNA PARIS
MELBOURNE SYDNEY AUCKLAND SINGAPORE TOKYO
IBADAN NAIROBI HARARE GABORONE PORTSMOUTH NH (USA)

This edition first published 1996.
The publishers and Series Editor are indebted to James Reeves for his work as
Founding Editor of the original Poetry Bookshelf series.

10 9 8 7 6 5 4 3 2 1
2000 99 98 97 96

A catalogue record for this book is available from the British Library on request.
ISBN 0 435 15078 2

Cover design by The Point

Text design by Roger Davies

Typeset by Books Unlimited (Nottm)

Printed by Clays Ltd, St Ives plc

CONTENTS

Background

Critical Approaches

Appendix

Select Bibliography

Index of First Lines

INTRODUCTION

Lyrical Ballads was one of the most influential books in English literature. No other verse collection has had such an impact on the course of
English literature and the study of English which grew out of it. It is a
key text in the development of Romanticism.

Romanticism was the great shift in feeling and thought that took place
in Britain and Europe between 1770–1850. Its political roots were in the
revolutions of America (1776) and France (1789). It rejected the sceptical,
scientific, rational philosophy of much of eighteenth-century Europe.
Romanticism initially championed progressive causes. But centrally, it
projected and validated individual experience – the primacy of the self
and intense 'on the edge' experiences. Its keywords were 'Nature'
'Imagination' and 'Liberty'.

William Wordsworth,
1770-1850

Samuel Taylor Coleridge,
1772-1834

Wordsworth and Coleridge were first-genera-
tion Romantics who embodied these new cur-
rents of thought and feeling in *Lyrical Ballads*.
Their subject matter and style were not particularly new – in fact there were firm links with
earlier poets and the magazine poetry of the day
– but the poets' treatment of their subject matter
was different. They used dramatic narratives
handled with psychological realism in a non-
judgemental way. They have a deliberate honesty. William and Dorothy Wordsworth and
Coleridge tried to see and feel things freshly and
to involve the reader in a freshness and complexity of response. The deliberate mixture of genres
helps to do this. A lyric is a short personal poem.
A ballad is a long, rather impersonal, narrative.
By combining the two – by saturating a story
with feeling – the poets were presenting the
reader with complex texts, without any authorial
mediation between subject and reader. Some
contemporary readers found this rather baffling.

Modern readers still find *Lyrical Ballads*
baffling. The reflective, blank verse meditations
(for example *The Nightingale*, *Tintern Abbey*), al-

though complex, are ultimately accessible. But the supernatural narratives and the tales of social realism can still present problems.

You need to be prepared to go beyond yourself and your own historical moment to enjoy these poems, which require some awareness of the contexts in which they were written and understood. The **Background** will help here, as will **1797–8: The Year of the** *Lyrical Ballads* and the **Appendix**, which contains examples of magazine poetry dealing with the same issues as *Lyrical Ballads*.

LYRICAL BALLADS

with

A FEW OTHER POEMS

BRISTOL
Printed by Biggs and Cottle
For T.N. Longman, Paternoster-Row, London

1798

Advertisement

Wordsworth wrote the Advertisement, with Coleridge's agreement, and it forms the nucleus of the Romantic debate on poetry which was developed through Wordsworth's Prefaces to later editions of *Lyrical Ballads* (1800, 1802) and Coleridge's *Biographia Literaria* (1817). See **Cultural and Literary Background**.

The tone of the Advertisement is both defensive and provocative. Wordsworth is very aware of the challenging nature of both subject matter and style. He defends the poems as 'experiments' in language and attacks the exaggerated poetic diction of conventional eighteenth-century poetry.

The keyword in the Advertisement is 'natural'. Wordsworth demands that the reader ask if the poems are a *natural* description of human passions. Here, he posits a term central to Romanticism.

Advertisement

IT is the honourable characteristic of Poetry that its materials are to be found in every subject which can interest the human mind. The evidence of this fact is to be sought, not in the writings of Critics, but in those of Poets themselves.

5 The majority of the following poems are to be considered as experiments. They were written chiefly with a view to ascertain how far the language of conversation in the middle and lower classes of society is adapted to the purposes of poetic pleasure. Readers accustomed to the gaudiness and inane phraseology of
10 many modern writers, if they persist in reading this book to its conclusion, will perhaps frequently have to struggle with feelings of strangeness and aukwardness: they will look round for poetry, and will be induced to enquire by what species of courtesy these attempts can be permitted to assume that title. It is desirable that
15 such readers, for their own sakes, should not suffer the solitary word Poetry, a word of very disputed meaning, to stand in the way of their gratification; but that, while they are perusing this book, they should ask themselves if it contains a natural delineation of human passions, human characters, and human incidents; and if
20 the answer be favourable to the author's wishes, that they should consent to be pleased in spite of that most dreadful enemy to our pleasures, our own pre-established codes of decision.

Readers of superior judgment may disapprove of the style in which many of these pieces are executed it must be expected that
25 many lines and phrases will not exactly suit their taste. It will perhaps appear to them, that wishing to avoid the prevalent fault of the day, the author has sometimes descended too low, and that many of his expressions are too familiar, and not of sufficient dignity. It is apprehended, that the more conversant the reader is with
30 our elder writers, and with those in modern times who have been the most successful in painting manners and passions, the fewer complaints of this kind will he have to make.

An accurate taste in poetry, and in all the other arts, Sir Joshua Reynolds has observed, is an acquired talent, which can only be
35 produced by severe thought, and a long continued intercourse with the best models of composition. This is mentioned not with

so ridiculous a purpose as to prevent the most inexperienced
reader from judging for himself; but merely to temper the rashness
of decision, and to suggest that if poetry be a subject on which
40 much time has not been bestowed, the judgment may be erron-
eous, and that in many cases it necessarily will be so.

The tale of Goody Blake and Harry Gill is founded on a well-
authenticated fact which happened in Warwickshire. Of the other
poems in the collection, it may be proper to say that they are either
45 absolute inventions of the author, or facts which took place within
his personal observation or that of his friends. The poem of the
Thorn, as the reader will soon discover, is not supposed to be
spoken in the author's own person: the character of the loquacious
narrator will sufficiently show itself in the course of the story. The
50 Rime of the Ancyent Marinere was professedly written in imita-
tion of the *style*, as well as of the spirit of the elder poets; but with
a few exceptions, the Author believes that the language adopted in
it has been equally intelligible for these three last centuries. The
lines entitled Expostulation and Reply, and those which follow,
55 arose out of conversation with a friend who was somewhat unreasonably attached to modern books of moral philosophy.

55 *friend* – William Hazlitt (see note, page 230).

Lyrical Ballads

The Rime of the Ancyent Marinere

Coleridge's poem is the most famous in the collection. You will have come across references to it, or possibly used expressions such as 'It's like an albatross round my neck' which derive from the story. You may already have read a version of it in an anthology. The most readily available version is the one Coleridge published in 1817, which contains many changes and has a prose 'gloss' or advice to readers.

This is an early version of a poem that Coleridge worked on for years. Recent scholarship suggests that there may be a hundred versions of it. This one was written between November 1797 and March 1798 and was begun as a collaboration with Wordsworth, planned on a walking tour to Linton with William and his sister Dorothy. Wordsworth soon left the poem to Coleridge after contributing a couple of images (lines 19–20, 218) and the central idea of shooting the albatross. He had been reading Shelvocke's **A Voyage around the World by the way of the Great South Sea** (1726). Coleridge was particularly interested in sea voyages and books of travel, as well as recent adventures like the voyage of the Bounty and its Mutiny (1789). The 'Argument' suggests the genre of the sea voyage. Other influences were the Gothic horror stories popular at the time, and, of course, the old ballads which were gaining in popularity in the second half of the eighteenth century.

Part I

The Mariner describes the ship's voyage south across the equator towards polar regions where they are trapped by ice. The Albatross appears. The ice cracks and the ship escapes. The Crew, including the Mariner, befriend the bird. The Mariner shoots it.

The story of the Mariner is 'framed' by the story of the Wedding Guest being interrupted by this frightening figure and prevented from attending the wedding.

How a Ship having passed the Line was driven by Storms to the cold
  Country towards the South Pole; and how from thence she made
  her course to the tropical Latitude of the Great Pacific Ocean;
  and of the strange things that befell; and in what manner the
  Ancyent Marinere came back to his own Country.

The Rime of the Ancyent Marinere,

IN SEVEN PARTS

I

It is an ancyent Marinere,
  And he stoppeth one of three:
"By thy long grey beard and thy glittering eye
  "Now wherefore stoppest me?

5 "The Bridegroom's doors are open'd wide
  "And I am next of kin;
"The Guests are met, the Feast is set, –
  "May'st hear the merry din. –

But still he holds the wedding-guest –
10 There was a Ship, quoth he –
"Nay, if thou'st got a laughsome tale,
  "Marinere! come with me."

He holds him with his skinny hand,
  Quoth he, there was a Ship –
15 "Now get thee hence, thou grey-beard Loon!
  "Or my Staff shall make thee skip.

He holds him with his glittering eye –
  The wedding guest stood still
And listens like a three year's child;
20 The Marinere hath his will.

21 *sate* – sat.

22 *chuse* – choose.

27 *Kirk* – church.

48 *Chaff* – the husks left after grain has been threshed.

The wedding-guest sate on a stone,
  He cannot chuse but hear:
And thus spake on that ancyent man,
  The bright-eyed Marinere.

25 The Ship was cheer'd, the Harbour clear'd –
  Merrily did we drop
Below the Kirk, below the Hill,
  Below the Light-house top.

The Sun came up upon the left,
30 Out of the Sea came he:
And he shone bright, and on the right
  Went down into the Sea.

Higher and higher every day,
  Till over the mast at noon –
35 The wedding-guest here beat his breast,
  For he heard the loud bassoon.

The Bride hath pac'd into the Hall,
  Red as a rose is she;
Nodding their heads before her goes
40 The merry Minstralsy.

The wedding-guest he beat his breast,
  Yet he cannot chuse but hear:
And thus spake on that ancyent Man,
  The bright-eyed Marinere.

45 Listen, Stranger! Storm and Wind,
  A Wind and Tempest strong!
For days and weeks it play'd us freaks –
  Like Chaff we drove along.

50 *cauld* – cold. Coleridge borrowed this and many other archaisms (old forms) from the traditional ballads.

53 *clifts* – cliffs.

55 *ken* – know, recognize.

60 *swound* – swoon or fainting-fit.

63 *an* – as if.

65 *biscuit-worms* – worms found in ships' biscuit crumbs. This sort of detail links the story with sea voyages such as Magellan's. It was deleted from later versions of the poem.

74 *vespers* – evening service in Roman Catholic and Church of England churches.

Listen, Stranger! Mist and Snow,
50   And it grew wond'rous cauld:
And Ice mast-high came floating by
      As green as Emerauld.

And thro' the drifts the snowy clifts
      Did send a dismal sheen;
55 Ne shapes of men ne beasts we ken –
      The Ice was all between.

The Ice was here, the Ice was there,
      The Ice was all around:
It crack'd and growl'd, and roar'd and howl'd –
60   Like noises of a swound.

At length did cross an Albatross,
      Thorough the Fog it came;
And an it were a Christian Soul,
      We hail'd it in God's name.

65 The Marineres gave it biscuit-worms,
      And round and round it flew:
The Ice did split with a Thunder-fit;
      The Helmsman steer'd us thro'.

And a good south wind sprung up behind,
70   The Albatross did follow;
And every day for food or play
      Came to the Marinere's hollo!

In mist or cloud on mast or shroud
      It perch'd for vespers nine,
75 Whiles all the night thro' fog-smoke white
      Glimmer'd the white moon-shine.

> *Why does the Mariner prevent a man from attending a wedding?*
>
> *Do you feel that events in Part I have natural or supernatural causes? Is the 'atmosphere' natural or supernatural?*
>
> *Why do the Crew hail the bird as a 'Christian soul'?*
>
> *Why does the Mariner shoot the Albatross?*

Part II

Part II describes the ship becalmed in the Pacific. The Crew suffer from drought and, possibly, hallucinations. A 'Spirit' enters their dreams. He has followed them from the 'land of mist and snow' and 'plagues' them. The sailors hang the corpse of the Albatross round the Mariner's neck.

83   *weft* – signal flag.

"God save thee, ancyent Marinere!
    "From the fiends that plague thee thus –
"Why look'st thou so?" – with my cross bow
80   I shot the Albatross.

II

The Sun came up upon the right,
    Out of the Sea came he;
And broad as a weft upon the left
    Went down into the Sea.

85   And the good south wind still blew behind,
    But no sweet Bird did follow
Ne any day for food or play
    Came to the Marinere's hollo!

And I had done an hellish thing
90   And it would work 'em woe:
For all averr'd, I had kill'd the Bird
    That made the Breeze to blow.

Ne dim ne red, like God's own head,
    The glorious Sun uprist:
95   Then all averr'd, I had kill'd the Bird
    That brought the fog and mist.

"Twas right, said they, such birds to slay
    That bring the fog and mist.

The breezes blew, the white foam flew,
100   The furrow follow'd free:
We were the first that ever burst
    Into that silent Sea.

123   *reel and rout* – wild dances.

125   *like a witch's oils* – Captain Cook describes the effects of phosphorescence like this.

129   *fathom* – a nautical measure of depth (6 feet).

Down dropt the breeze, the Sails dropt down,
    'Twas sad as sad could be
105 And we did speak only to break
    The silence of the Sea.

All in a hot and copper sky
    The bloody sun at noon,
Right up above the mast did stand,
110   No bigger than the moon.

Day after day, day after day,
    We stuck, ne breath ne motion,
As idle as a painted Ship
    Upon a painted Ocean.

115 Water, water, every where
    And all the boards did shrink;
Water, water, every where
    Ne any drop to drink.

The very deeps did rot: O Christ!
120   That ever this should be!
Yea, slimy things did crawl with legs
    Upon the slimy Sea.

About, about, in reel and rout
    The Death-fires danc'd at night;
125 The water, like a witch's oils,
    Burnt green and blue and white.

And some in dreams assured were
    Of the Spirit that plagued us so:
Nine fathom deep he had follow'd us
130   From the Land of Mist and Snow.

Why do the Crew change their minds?

Find imagery that relates to death, stasis and dumbness.

Why do the Crew hang the Albatross round the Mariner's neck?
What is its relation to the Cross? What does the bird now signify?

The narrative moves between the natural and the supernatural here, and
between the conscious and the unconscious. What image does Coleridge
use to convey this?

Part III

Here spirits directly invade the sailors' world of drought and horror. A
spectral ship sails towards them at sunset without help from wind or tide.
The ship contains two spectres who are playing at dice. The female wins.
The Crew die cursing the Mariner.

144   *wist* – was aware of.

146   *ner'd* – drew nearer.

152   *I bit my arm and suck'd the blood* – Coleridge was in the habit, when he
      ran out of ink, of biting his thumb and writing in blood.

160   *to work us weal* – to do us any good.

And every tongue thro' utter drouth
    Was wither'd at the root;
We could not speak no more than if
    We had been choked with soot.

135 Ah wel-a-day! what evil looks
    Had I from old and young;
Instead of the Cross the Albatross
    About my neck was hung.

III

I saw a something in the Sky
140   No bigger than my fist;
At first it seem'd a little speck
    And then it seem'd a mist:
It mov'd and mov'd, and took at last
    A certain shape, I wist.

145 A speck, a mist, a shape, I wist!
    And still it ner'd and ner'd;
And, an it dodg'd a water-sprite,
    It plung'd and tack'd and veer'd.

With throat unslack'd, with black lips bak'd
150   Ne could we laugh, ne wail:
Then while thro' drouth all dumb they stood
I bit my arm and suck'd the blood
    And cry'd, A sail! a sail!

With throat unslack'd, with black lips bak'd
155   Agape they hear'd me call:
Gramercy! they for joy did grin
And all at once their breath drew in
    As they were drinking all.

She doth not tack from side to side –
160   Hither to work us weal
Withouten wind, withouten tide
    She steddies with upright keel.

170 *Heaven's mother* – the Virgin Mary.

176 *gossameres* – fine cobwebs.

180 *Pheere* – companion.

182 *ween* – believe, judge.

184 *charnel crust* – the decay of the grave.

The western wave was all a flame,
   The day was well nigh done!
165 Almost upon the western wave
   Rested the broad bright Sun;
When that strange shape drove suddenly
   Betwixt us and the Sun.
And strait the Sun was fleck'd with bars
170 (Heaven's mother send us grace)
As if thro' a dungeon grate he peer'd
   With broad and burning face.

Alas! (thought I, and my heart beat loud)
   How fast she neres and neres!
175 Are those *her* Sails that glance in the Sun
   Like restless gossameres?

Are these *her* naked ribs, which fleck'd
   The sun that did behind them peer?
And are these two all, all the crew,
180 That woman and her fleshless Pheere?

His bones were black with many a crack,
   All black and bare, I ween;
Jet-black and bare, save where with rust
Of mouldy damps and charnel crust
185 They're patch'd with purple and green.

Her lips are red, *her* looks are free,
   Her locks are yellow as gold:
Her skin is as white as leprosy,
And she is far liker Death than he;
190 Her flesh makes the still air cold.

195 *sterte* – started.

201 *clombe* – climbed.

207 *ee* – eye.

What is the dominant colour of this part of the poem? Why?

Why do the spectres play at dice? What are they playing for? Is it for the Crew or the Mariner? What does this suggest about the nature of justice in the Mariner's universe?

Or is the ship a hallucination? If so, what does the dice game suggest about the Mariner's sense of justice? Why does Coleridge deliberately introduce an element of chance here?

What have the sailors done to deserve their deaths? Why does the Mariner get this particular punishment?

Can you find any particular significance in the images of the sun and moon in this section?

Part IV

This is the crisis and turning-point for the Mariner. For seven days and nights he is in a state of moral and emotional paralysis, unable to pray, surrounded by the dead. He watches the moon's progress through the sky. Then, watching the water snakes, he blesses them 'unaware'. At this the Albatross falls from his neck into the sea.

The naked Hulk alongside came
    And the Twain were playing dice;
"The Game is done! I've won, I've won!"
    Quoth she, and whistled thrice.

195 A gust of wind sterte up behind
    And whistled thro' his bones;
Thro' the holes of his eyes and the hole of his mouth
    Half-whistles and half-groans.

With never a whisper in the Sea
200   Off darts the Spectre-ship;
While clombe above the Eastern bar
The horned Moon, with one bright Star
    Almost atween the tips.

One after one by the horned Moon
205   (Listen, O Stranger! to me)
Each turn'd his face with a ghastly pang
    And curs'd me with his ee.

Four times fifty living men,
    With never a sigh or groan,
210 With heavy thump, a lifeless lump
    They dropp'd down one by one.

Their souls did from their bodies fly, –
    They fled to bliss or woe;
And every soul it pass'd me by,
215   Like the whiz of my Cross-bow.

IV

"I fear thee, ancyent Marinere!
  "I fear thy skinny hand;
"And thou art long and lank and brown
  "As is the ribb'd Sea-sand.

234   *eldritch* – hideous and ghostly.

220 "I fear thee and thy glittering eye
     "And thy skinny hand so brown –
   Fear not, fear not, thou wedding guest!
     This body dropt not down.

   Alone, alone, all all alone
225   Alone on the wide wide Sea;
   And Christ would take no pity on
     My soul in agony.

   The many men so beautiful,
     And they all dead did lie!
230 And a million million slimy things
     Liv'd on – and so did I.

   I look'd upon the rotting Sea,
     And drew my eyes away;
   I look'd upon the eldritch deck,
235   And there the dead men lay.

   I look'd to Heaven, and try'd to pray;
     But or ever a prayer had gusht,
   A wicked whisper came and made
     My heart as dry as dust.

240 I clos'd my lids and kept them close,
     Till the balls like pulses beat;
   For the sky and the sea, and the sea and the sky
   Lay like a load on my weary eye,
     And the dead were at my feet.

245 The cold sweat melted from their limbs,
     Ne rot, ne reek did they;
   The look with which they look'd on me,
     Had never pass'd away.

Read lines 119–26 again and compare them with lines 264–73. What causes the Mariner's change of attitude to the water snakes?

Why does a spring of love gush from his heart? How can he bless the water snakes 'unaware'? Is it intentional or unintentional?

An orphan's curse would drag to Hell
250   A spirit from on high:
But O! more horrible than that
    Is the curse in a dead man's eye!
Seven days, seven nights I saw that curse,
    And yet I could not die.

255 The moving Moon went up the sky
        And no where did abide:
    Softly she was going up
        And a star or two beside –

    Her beams bemock'd the sultry main
260   Like morning frost yspread;
    But where the ship's huge shadow lay,
    The charmed water burnt alway
        A still and awful red.

    Beyond the shadow of the ship
265 I   watch'd the water-snakes:
    They mov'd in tracks of shining white;
    And when they rear'd, the elfish light
        Fell off in hoary flakes.

    Within the shadow of the ship
230   I watch'd their rich attire:
    Blue, glossy green, and velvet black
    They coil'd and swam; and every track
        Was a flash of golden fire.

    O happy living things! no tongue
275   Their beauty might declare:
    A spring of love gusht from my heart,
        And I bless'd them unaware!
    Sure my kind saint took pity on me,
        And I bless'd them unaware.

Part V

The Mariner sleeps and the rain comes. It seems, at this point, as if the narrative could close, but this proves not to be the case. The Mariner wakes to a strange storm in the sky which does not move the sails; the dead men rise up, work the ropes and sing together round the mast. The Mariner feels excluded and ghost-like. The ship moves through the agency of the Polar Spirit. In a faint, the Mariner hears two Spirits and learns of his own transgression and that more 'penance' is due.

286   *Mary-queen* – Mary, the mother of God. The moon is also seen as a representative of the mother.

286   *yeven* – given.

289   *silly* – homely.

304   *sere* – dry, shrivelled.

306   *fire-flags* – Aurora Borealis.

280　The self-same moment I could pray;
　　　And from my neck so free
　　　The Albatross fell off, and sank
　　　　Like lead into the sea.

V

　　　O sleep, it is a gentle thing
285　　Belov'd from pole to pole!
　　　To Mary-queen the praise be yeven
　　　She sent the gentle sleep from heaven
　　　　That slid into my soul.

　　　The silly buckets on the deck
290　　That had so long remain'd,
　　　I dreamt that they were fill'd with dew
　　　　And when I awoke it rain'd.

　　　My lips were wet, my throat was cold,
　　　　My garments all were dank;
295　Sure I had drunken in my dreams
　　　　And still my body drank.

　　　I mov'd and could not feel my limbs,
　　　　I was so light, almost
　　　I thought that I had died in sleep,
300　　And was a blessed Ghost.

　　　The roaring wind! it roar'd far off,
　　　　It did not come anear;
　　　But with its sound it shook the sails
　　　　That were so thin and sere.

305　The upper air bursts into life,
　　　　And a hundred fire-flags sheen
　　　To and fro they are hurried about;
　　　And to and fro, and in and out
　　　　The stars dance on between.

311 *sedge* – reeds.

310 The coming wind doth roar more loud;
      The sails do sigh, like sedge:
    The rain pours down from one black cloud
      And the Moon is at its edge.

    Hark! hark! the thick black cloud is cleft,
315   And the Moon is at its side:
    Like waters shot from some high crag,
    The lightning falls with never a jag
      A river steep and wide.

    The strong wind reach'd the ship: it roar'd
320   And dropp'd down, like a stone!
    Beneath the lightning and the moon
      The dead men gave a groan.

    They groan'd, they stirr'd, they all uprose,
      Ne spake, ne mov'd their eyes:
325 It had been strange, even in a dream
      To have seen those dead men rise.

    The helmsman steerd, the ship mov'd on;
      Yet never a breeze up-blew;
    The Marineres all 'gan work the ropes,
330   Where they were wont to do:
    They rais'd their limbs like lifeless tools –
      We were a ghastly crew.

    The body of my brother's son
      Stood by me knee to knee:
335 The body and I pull'd at one rope,
      But he said nought to me –
    And I quak'd to think of my own voice
      How frightful it would be!

348   *Lavrock* – skylark.

351   *jargoning* – birdsong.

What does the music signify?

The day-light dawn'd – they dropp'd their arms,
340   And cluster'd round the mast:
Sweet sounds rose slowly thro' their mouths
    And from their bodies pass'd.

Around, around, flew each sweet sound,
    Then darted to the sun:
345 Slowly the sounds came back again
    Now mix'd, now one by one.

Sometimes a dropping from the sky
    I heard the Lavrock sing;
Sometimes all little birds that are
350 How they seem'd to fill the sea and air
    With their sweet jargoning,

And now 'twas like all instruments,
    Now like a lonely flute;
And now it is an angel's song
355   That makes the heavens be mute.

It ceas'd: yet still the sails made on
    A pleasant noise till noon,
A noise like of a hidden brook
    In the leafy month of June,
360 That to the sleeping woods all night
    Singeth a quiet tune.

Listen, O listen, thou Wedding-guest!
    "Marinere! thou hast thy will:
"For that, which comes out of thine eye, doth make
365   "My body and soul to be still."

375 *n'old* – would not.

Never sadder tale was told
    To a man of woman born:
Sadder and wiser thou wedding-guest!
    Thou'lt rise to morrow morn.

370 Never sadder tale was heard
    By a man of woman born:
The Marineres all return'd to work
    As silent as beforne.

The Marineres all 'gan pull the ropes,
375   But look at me they n'old:
Thought I, I am as thin as air –
    They cannot me behold.

Till noon we silently sail'd on
    Yet never a breeze did breathe:
380 Slowly and smoothly went the ship
    Mov'd onward from beneath.

Under the keel nine fathom deep
    From the land of mist and snow
The spirit slid: and it was He
385   That made the Ship to go.
The sails at noon left off their tune
    And the Ship stood still also.

The sun right up above the mast
    Had fix'd her to the ocean:
390 But in a minute she 'gan stir
    With a short uneasy motion –
Backwards and forwards half her length
    With a short uneasy motion.

Then, like a pawing horse let go,
395   She made a sudden bound:

397 swound – faint.

> What does penance mean in this context?

> Why does the Mariner have to do more penance?

Part VI

When the Spirits have finished speaking, the Mariner wakes up to find the entire Crew staring at him accusingly. He seems unable to escape the Crew's curse. He recognizes that the ship is sailing into his own harbour. He hears the Pilot's boat approaching and sees the Hermit on board. The Mariner immediately thinks that the Hermit will hear his confession and absolve him of his crime ('shrive' him).

It flung the blood into my head,
  And I fell into a swound.

How long in that same fit I lay,
  I have not to declare;
400 But ere my living life return'd,
I heard and in my soul discern'd
    Two voices in the air,

"Is it he? quoth one, "Is this the man
  "By him who died on cross,
405 "With his cruel bow he lay'd full low
  "The harmless Albatross.

"The spirit who 'bideth by himself
  "In the land of mist and snow,
"He lov'd the bird that lov'd the man
410   "Who shot him with his bow.

The other was a softer voice,
  As soft as honey-dew:
Quoth he the man hath penance done,
  And penance more will do.

VI
FIRST VOICE
415 "But tell me, tell me! speak again,
  "Thy soft response renewing –
"What makes that ship drive on so fast?
  "What is the Ocean doing?

SECOND VOICE
"Still as a Slave before his Lord,
420   "The Ocean hath no blast:
"His great bright eye most silently
  "Up to the moon is cast –

Why hasn't the curse died away?

Why can't the Mariner pray (again)?

445 *een* – eyes.

"If he may know which way to go,
  "For she guides him smooth or grim,
425 "See, brother, see! how graciously
  "She looketh down on him.

FIRST VOICE

"But why drives on that ship so fast
  "Withouten wave or wind
SECOND VOICE
"The air is cut away before,
430 "And closes from behind.

"Fly, brother, fly! more high, more high,
  "Or we shall be belated:
"For slow and slow that ship will go,
  "When the Marinere's trance is abated."

435 I woke, and we were sailing on
  As in a gentle weather:
"Twas night, calm night, the moon was high:
  The dead men stood together.

All stood together on the deck,
440 For a charnel-dungeon fitter:
All fix'd on me their stony eyes
  That in the moon did glitter.

The pang, the curse, with which they died,
  Had never pass'd away:
445 I could not draw my een from theirs
  Ne turn them up to pray.

And in its time the spell was snapt,
  And I could move my een:

I look'd far-forth, but little saw
450   Of what might else be seen.

Like one, that on a lonely road
    Doth walk in fear and dread,
And having once turn'd round, walks on
    And turns no more his head:
455 Because he knows, a frightful fiend
    Doth close behind him tread.

But soon there breath'd a wind on me,
    Ne sound ne motion made:
Its path was not upon the sea
460   In ripple or in shade.

It rais'd my hair, it fann'd my cheek,
    Like a meadow-gale of spring –
It mingled strangely with my fears,
    Yet it felt like a welcoming.

465 Swiftly, swiftly flew the ship,
    Yet she sail'd softly too:
Sweetly, sweetly blew the breeze –
    On me alone it blew.

O dream of joy! is this indeed
470   The light-house top I see?
Is this the Hill? Is this the Kirk?
    Is this mine own countrée?

We drifted o'er the Harbour-bar,
    And I with sobs did pray –
"O let me be awake, my God!
    "Or let me sleep alway!"

490 *rood* – the Cross.

The harbour-bay was clear as glass,
　　So smoothly it was strewn!
And on the bay the moon light lay,
480　　And the shadow of the moon.

The moonlight bay was white all o'er,
　　Till rising from the same,
Full many shapes, that shadows were,
　　Like as of torches came.

485 A little distance from the prow
　　Those dark-red shadows were;
But soon I saw that my own flesh
　　Was red as in a glare.

I turn'd my head in fear and dread,
490　　And by the holy rood,
The bodies had advanc'd, and now
　　Before the mast they stood.

They lifted up their stiff right arms,
　　They held them strait and tight;
495 And each right-arm burnt like a torch,
　　A torch that's borne upright.
Their stony eye-balls glitter'd on
　　In the red and smoky light.

I pray'd and turn'd my head away
500　　Forth looking as before.
There was no breeze upon the bay,
　　No wave against the shore.

The rock shone bright, the kirk no less
　　That stands above the rock:
505 The moonlight steep'd in silentness
　　The steady weathercock.

515 *corse* – corpse.

517 *seraph-man* – angel.

527 *Eftsones* – but soon.

The Crew are presented in four different transformations in this section. Why?

And the bay was white with silent light,
    Till rising from the same
Full many shapes, that shadows were,
510   In crimson colours came.

A little distance from the prow
    Those crimson shadows were:
I turn'd my eyes upon the deck –
    O Christ! what saw I there!
515 Each corse lay flat, lifeless and flat;
    And by the Holy rood
A man all light, a seraph-man,
    On every corse there stood.

This seraph-band, each wav'd his hand:
520   It was a heavenly sight:
They stood as signals to the land,
    Each one a lovely light:

This seraph-band, each wav'd his hand,
    No voice did they impart –
525 No voice; but O! the silence sank,
    Like music on my heart.

Eftsones I heard the dash of oars,
    I heard the pilot's cheer:
My head was turn'd perforce away
530   And I saw a boat appear.

Then vanish'd all the lovely lights;
    The bodies rose anew:
With silent pace, each to his place,
    Came back the ghastly crew.
535 The wind, that shade nor motion made,
    On me alone it blew.

540   *blast* – destroy.

> *Why does the Mariner think the Hermit can 'shrive' him? Does he do this?*

Part VII

The Mariner listens to the voices from the Pilot's boat. They are frightened by the ship's ghostly appearance. A terrible rumbling is heard beneath the water and the ship sinks. The Mariner finds himself in the Pilot's boat. He begs the Hermit to shrive him and is 'wrenched with a woeful agony' to tell his tale.

Here the Mariner resembles traditional figures like Cain or the Wandering Jew, doomed to wander the earth. He has to teach the importance of love and reverence for all things.

> *This is the 'moral' of the ballad, but there is so much anguish here that this seemingly 'naive' conclusion should perhaps be questioned. What do you understand by lines 630–34? (This suggestion of real doubt and hopelessness was most unusual at the time.)*

357   *trow* – think, believe.

563   *sere* – dry, withered.

The pilot, and the pilot's boy
    I heard them coming fast:
Dear Lord in Heaven! it was a joy,
540   The dead men could not blast.

I saw a third – I heard his voice:
    It is the Hermit good!
He singeth loud his godly hymns
    That he makes in the wood.
545   He'll shrieve my soul, he'll wash away
    The Albatross's blood.

VII

This Hermit good lives in that wood
    Which slopes down to the Sea.
How loudly his sweet voice he rears!
550   He loves to talk with Marineres
    That come from a far Contrée.

He kneels at morn and noon and eve –
    He hath a cushion plump:
It is the moss, that wholly hides
555   The rotted old Oak-stump.

The Skiff-boat ne'rd: I heard them talk,
    "Why, this is strange, I trow!
"Where are those lights so many and fair
    "That signal made but now?

560 "Strange, by my faith! the Hermit said –
    "And they answer'd not our cheer.
"The planks look warp'd, and see those sails
    "How thin they are and sere!
"I never saw aught like to them
565   "Unless perchance it were

"The skeletons of leaves that lag
    "My forest brook along:
"When the Ivy-tod is heavy with snow,
"And the Owlet whoops to the wolf below
570   "That eats the she-wolf's young.

"Dear Lord! it has a fiendish look –
    (The Pilot made reply)
"I am a-fear'd. – "Push on, push on!
    "Said the Hermit cheerily.

575 The Boat came closer to the Ship,
        But I ne spake ne stirr'd!
    The Boat came close beneath the Ship,
        And strait a sound was heard!

    Under the water it rumbled on,
580   Still louder and more dread:
    It reach'd the Ship, it split the bay;
        The Ship went down like lead.

    Stunn'd by that loud and dreadful sound,
        Which sky and ocean smote:
585 Like one that hath been seven days drown'd
        My body lay afloat:
    But, swift as dreams, myself I found
        Within the Pilot's boat.

    Upon the whirl, where sank the Ship,
590   The boat spun round and round:
    And all was still, save that the hill
        Was telling of the sound.

    I mov'd my lips: the Pilot shriek'd
        And fell down in a fit.

Why does the Mariner have to tell his tale? Has he been forgiven? Why does the need to tell it return?

595 The Holy Hermit rais'd his eyes
        And pray'd where he did sit.

    I took the oars: the Pilot's boy,
        Who now doth crazy go,
    Laugh'd loud and long, and all the while
600   His eyes went to and fro,
    "Ha! ha!" quoth he – "full plain I see,
        "The devil knows how to row."
    And now all in mine own Countrée
        I stood on the firm land!
605 The Hermit stepp'd forth from the boat,
        And scarcely he could stand.

    "O shrieve me, shrieve me, holy Man!
        The Hermit cross'd his brow –
    "Say quick," quoth he, "I bid thee say
610   "What manner man art thou?

    Forthwith this frame of mine was wrench'd
        With a woeful agony,
    Which forc'd me to begin my tale
        And then it left me free.

615 Since then at an uncertain hour
        Now oftimes and now fewer,
    That anguish comes and makes me tell
        My ghastly aventure.

    I pass, like night, from land to land;
620   I have strange power of speech;
    The moment that his face I see
    I know the man that must hear me;
        To him my tale I teach.

Why is it sweeter for the Mariner to pray with the congregation than to attend a wedding feast?

What loud uproar bursts from that door!
625　　The Wedding-guests are there;
But in the Garden-bower the Bride
　　And Bride-maids singing are:
And hark the little Vesper-bell
　　Which biddeth me to prayer.

630　O Wedding-guest! this soul hath been
　　Alone on a wide wide sea
So lonely 'twas, that God himself
　　Scarce seemed there to be.

O sweeter than the Marriage-feast,
635　　'Tis sweeter far to me
To walk together to the Kirk
　　With a goodly company.

To walk together to the Kirk
　　And all together pray,
640　While each to his great father bends,
Old men, and babes, and loving friends,
　　And Youths, and Maidens gay.

Farewel, farewell! but this I tell
　　To thee, thou wedding-guest!
645　He prayeth well who loveth well
　　Both man and bird and beast.

He prayeth best who loveth best,
　　All things both great and small:
For the dear God, who loveth us,
650　　He made and loveth all.

The Marinere, whose eye is bright,
　　Whose beard with age is hoar,

The Foster-Mother's Tale

This is an extract from Coleridge's play *Osorio* (1797). The story told here has nothing to do with the plot of the play and was later cut out. Coleridge's biographer Holmes suggests that this is a 'fictional sketch' of Coleridge's brother Frank, who served in India. Frank was wounded at Seringapatam and, delirious with fever, shot himself at the age of twenty-two in 1792. If this is the case, Coleridge has transformed the gallant ensign of infantry into a particular sort of Romantic figure.

The Foster-Mother is prompted to tell her tale because Maria has been troubled by 'wilder fancies' through a story told by a 'strange man'. The Foster-Mother describes a baby found under a tree who grows up into a pretty but 'most unteachable boy'. He is first left to Nature and then taught by a Friar. Isolated and reading too much, he becomes heretical in his thinking and is put in prison. He manages to escape and sails to America where he disappears into the wilderness, presumably to live and die 'among the savage men'.

Is gone; and now the wedding-guest
  Turn'd from the bridegroom's door.

655 He went, like one that hath been stunn'd
  And is of sense forlorn:
A sadder and a wiser man
  He rose the morrow morn.

The Foster-Mother's Tale,

A DRAMATIC FRAGMENT

FOSTER-MOTHER

I never saw the man whom you describe.

MARIA

'Tis strange! he spake of you familiarly
As mine and Albert's common Foster-mother.

FOSTER-MOTHER

Now blessings on the man, whoe'er he be,
5 That joined your names with mine! O my sweet lady,
As often as I think of those dear times
When you two little ones would stand at eve
On each side of my chair, and make me learn
All you had learnt in the day; and how to talk
10 In gentle phrase, then bid me sing to you –
'Tis more like heaven to come than what *has* been.

MARIA

O my dear Mother! this strange man has left me
Troubled with wilder fancies, than the moon
Breeds in the love-sick maid who gazes at it,
15 Till lost in inward vision, with wet eye
She gazes idly! – But that entrance, Mother!

28 *Lord Velez* – character in *Osorio*.

31 *told a bead* – counted his rosary (a string of beads used by Roman
    Catholics as an *aide-memoire* for private prayers).

37 *simples* – medicinal herbs.

FOSTER-MOTHER

Can no one hear? It is a perilous tale!

MARIA

No one.

FOSTER-MOTHER

My husband's father told it me,
20 Poor old Leoni! – Angels rest his soul!
He was a woodman, and could fell and saw
With lusty arm. You know that huge round beam
Which props the hanging wall of the old chapel?
Beneath that tree, while yet it was a tree
25 He found a baby wrapt in mosses, lined
With thistle-beards, and such small locks of wool
As hang on brambles. Well, he brought him home,
And reared him at the then Lord Velez' cost
And so the babe grew up a pretty boy,
30 A pretty boy, but most unteachable –
And never learnt a prayer, nor told a bead,
But knew the names of birds, and mocked their notes,
And whistled, as he were a bird himself:
And all the autumn 'twas his only play
35 To get the seeds of wild flowers, and to plant them
With earth and water, on the stumps of trees.
A Friar, who gathered simples in the wood,
A grey-haired man – he loved this little boy,
The boy loved him – and, when the Friar taught him,
40 He soon could write with the pen: and from that time,
Lived chiefly at the Convent or the Castle.
So he became a very learned youth.
But Oh! poor wretch! – he read, and read, and read,
'Till his brain turned – and ere his twentieth year,
45 He had unlawful thoughts of many things:

Compare the upbringing of Maria (and Albert) with the upbringing of the foundling boy. What has he lacked? What has he gained?

And though he prayed, he never loved to pray
With holy men, nor in a holy place –
But yet his speech, it was so soft and sweet,
The late Lord Velez ne'er was wearied with him.
50   And once, as by the north side of the Chapel
They stood together, chained in deep discourse,
The earth heaved under them with such a groan,
That the wall tottered, and had well-nigh fallen
Right on their heads. My Lord was sorely frightened;
55   A fever seized him, and he made confession
Of all the heretical and lawless talk
Which brought this judgment: so the youth was seized
And cast into that hole. My husband's father
Sobbed like a child – it almost broke his heart:
60   And once as he was working in the cellar,
He heard a voice distinctly; 'twas the youth's,
Who sung a doleful song about green fields,
How sweet it were on lake or wild savannah,
To hunt for food, and be a naked man,
65   And wander up and down at liberty.
He always doted on the youth, and now
His love grew desperate; and defying death,
He made that cunning entrance I described:
And the young man escaped.

MARIA

70   'Tis a sweet tale:
Such as would lull a listening child to sleep,
His rosy face besoiled with unwiped tears. –
And what became of him?

FOSTER-MOTHER
He went on ship-board

Lines
left upon a Seat in a Yew-tree which stands near
the Lake of Esthwaite, on a desolate part of the shore,
yet commanding a beautiful prospect

Wordsworth began this poem in 1795 and finished it early in 1797. He was
at school at Hawkshead on Lake Esthwaite in the Lake District, and he later
said that the character in the poem was 'a gentleman of the neighbourhood,
a man of talent and learning, who had been educated at one of our
Universities, and returned to pass his time in seclusion on his own estate. He
died a bachelor in middle age'.

3   *rivulet* – stream.

3   *verdant* – fertile.

75 With those bold voyagers, who made discovery
    Of golden lands. Leoni's younger brother
    Went likewise, and when he returned to Spain,
    He told Leoni, that the poor mad youth,
    Soon after they arrived in that new world,
80 In spite of his dissuasion, seized a boat,
    And all alone, set sail by silent moonlight
    Up a great river, great as any sea,
    And ne'er was heard of more: but 'tis supposed,
    He lived and died among the savage men. –

Lines

left upon a Seat in a Yew-tree which stands near the Lake of Esthwaite, on a desolate part of the shore, yet commanding a beautiful prospect

         – Nay, Traveller! rest. This lonely yew-tree stands
         Far from all human dwelling: what if here
         No sparkling rivulet spread the verdant herb;
         What if these barren boughs the bee not loves;
    5   Yet, if the wind breathe soft, the curling waves,
         That break against the shore, shall lull thy mind
         By one soft impulse saved from vacancy.

                                  Who he was
         That piled these stones, and with the mossy sod
    10   First covered o'er, and taught this aged tree,
         Now wild, to bend its arms in circling shade,
         I well remember. – He was one who own'd
         No common soul. In youth, by genius nurs'd,
         And big with lofty views, he to the world
    15   Went forth, pure in his heart, against the taint
         Of dissolute tongues, 'gainst jealousy, and hate,
         And scorn, against all enemies prepared,
         All but neglect: and so, his spirit damped
         At once, with rash disdain he turned away,

Why does the solitary man leave the world and retire to this place?

What does he envy in others (lines 30–40)? How would you describe him?

20 And with the food of pride sustained his soul
In solitude. – Stranger! these gloomy boughs
Had charms for him; and here he loved to sit,
His only visitants a straggling sheep,
The stone-chat, or the glancing sand-piper;
25 And on these barren rocks, with juniper,
And heath, and thistle, thinly sprinkled o'er,
Fixing his downward eye, he many an hour
A morbid pleasure nourished, tracing here
An emblem of his own unfruitful life:
30 And lifting up his head, he then would gaze
On the more distant scene; how lovely 'tis
Thou seest, and he would gaze till it became
Far lovelier, and his heart could not sustain
The beauty still more beauteous. Nor, that time,
35 Would he forget those beings, to whose minds,
Warm from the labours of benevolence,
The world, and man himself, appeared a scene
Of kindred loveliness: then he would sigh
With mournful joy, to think that others felt
40 What he must never feel: and so, lost man!
On visionary views would fancy feed,
Till his eye streamed with tears. In this deep vale
He died, this seat his only monument.

If thou be one whose heart the holy forms
45 Of young imagination have kept pure,
Stranger! henceforth be warned; and know, that pride,
Howe'er disguised in its own majesty,
Is littleness; that he, who feels contempt
For any living thing, hath faculties
50 Which he has never used; that thought with him
Is in its infancy. The man, whose eye
Is ever on himself, doth look on one,
The least of nature's works, one who might move
The wise man to that scorn which wisdom holds
55 Unlawful, ever. O, be wiser thou!
Instructed that true knowledge leads to love,

59   *revere* – regard as sacred or exalted.

60   *lowliness* – humble, modest, unpretentious feelings.

> Wordsworth describes the solitary's particular fault and warns the reader against it. What is the fault? What effect does it have (lines 49–60)?

The Nightingale
A Conversational Poem
Written in April, 1798

Coleridge sent this poem to the Wordsworths on 10 May 1798. It is directly addressed to them (line 40) and re-enacts a night ramble they took to hear the nightingales at Dodington Hall. It reconstructs their literary conversation (they were talking about Milton's *Il Penseroso*); describes the birds and their song; introduces a Romantic female figure and then finishes 'at home' in Nether Stowey with a domestic anecdote about his son.

1   *relique* – remains.

7   *verdure* – green vegetation of Spring.

9   *vernal* – appearing in Spring.

> Why does the night-wandering man (line 16) find the nightingale's song melancholy?

True dignity abides with him alone
Who, in the silent hour of inward thought,
Can still suspect, and still revere himself,
60   In lowliness of heart.

The Nightingale;

A CONVERSATIONAL POEM,
Written in April, 1798

No cloud, no relique of the sunken day
Distinguishes the West, no long thin slip
Of sullen Light, no obscure trembling hues.
Come, we will rest on this old mossy Bridge!
5   You see the glimmer of the stream beneath,
But hear no murmuring: it flows silently
O'er its soft bed of verdure. All is still,
A balmy night! and tho' the stars be dim,
Yet let us think upon the vernal showers
10   That gladden the green earth, and we shall find
A pleasure in the dimness of the stars.
And hark! the Nightingale begins its song,
"Most musical, most melancholy" * Bird!
A melancholy Bird? O idle thought!
15   In nature there is nothing melancholy.
– But some night-wandering Man, whose heart was pierc'd
With the remembrance of a grievous wrong,
Or slow distemper or neglected love,
(And so, poor Wretch! fill'd all things with himself
20   And made all gentle sounds tell back the tale
Of his own sorrows) he and such as he

---

*   *'Most musical, most melancholy.'* This passage in Milton possesses an excellence far superior to that of mere description: it is spoken in the character of the melancholy Man, and has therefore a *dramatic* propriety. The Author makes this remark, to rescue himself from the charge of having alluded with levity to a line in Milton: a charge than which none could be more painful to him, except perhaps that of having ridiculed his Bible.

39 *Philomela* – this refers to a Greek legend. Philomela was raped by her sister's husband. He cut out her tongue, but she 'told' her story in her tapestry. She was turned into a nightingale.

48 *disburthen* – relieve, unload.

50 *a castle* – Enmore Castle near Stowey.

How should poets spend their time? Why?

Show how Coleridge replicates the song of the nightingale (lines 43–49, 82–86).

First nam'd these notes a melancholy strain;
And many a poet echoes the conceit,
Poet, who hath been building up the rhyme
25 When he had better far have stretch'd his limbs
Beside a brook in mossy forest-dell
By sun or moonlight, to the influxes
Of shapes and sounds and shifting elements
Surrendering his whole spirit, of his song
30 And of his fame forgetful! so his fame
Should share in nature's immortality,
A venerable thing! and so his song
Should make all nature lovelier, and itself
Be lov'd, like nature! – But 'twill not be so;
35 And youths and maidens most poetical
Who lose the deep'ning twilights of the spring
In ball-rooms and hot theatres, they still
Full of meek sympathy must heave their sighs
O'er Philomela's pity-pleading strains.
40 My Friend, and my Friend's Sister! we have learnt
A different lore: we may not thus profane
Nature's sweet voices always full of love
And joyance! 'Tis the merry Nightingale
That crowds, and hurries, and precipitates
45 With fast thick warble his delicious notes,
As he were fearful, that an April night
Would be too short for him to utter forth
His love-chant, and disburthen his full soul
Of all its music! And I know a grove
50 Of large extent, hard by a castle huge
Which the great lord inhabits not: and so
This grove is wild with tangling underwood,
And the trim walks are broken up, and grass,
Thin grass and king-cups grow within the paths.
55 But never elsewhere in one place I knew
So many Nightingales: and far and near
In wood and thicket over the wide grove

69 *love-torch* – the chemical phosphorescence of the glow-worm, designed to attract a mate.

69 *a most gentle maid* – Ellen Cruikshank, sister of a friend.

Who or what does the 'gentle maid' remind you of?

76 *What time* – whenever.

82 *airy harps* – Aeolian or wind harps. The harp was set in the open air for the wind to play. This was a favourite image for Coleridge and a very Romantic symbol, particularly of inspiration.

84 *blosmy* – flowering.

90 *strain* – melody.

They answer and provoke each other's songs –
With skirmish and capricious passagings,
60 And murmurs musical and swift jug jug
And one low piping sound more sweet than all –
Stirring the air with such an harmony,
That should you close your eyes, you might almost
Forget it was not day! On moonlight bushes,
65 Whose dewy leafits are but half disclos'd,
You may perchance behold them on the twigs,
Their bright, bright eyes, their eyes both bright and full,
Glistning, while many a glow-worm in the shade
Lights up her love-torch.

                    A most gentle maid
70 Who dwelleth in her hospitable home
Hard by the Castle, and at latest eve,
(Even like a Lady vow'd and dedicate
To something more than nature in the grove)
Glides thro' the pathways; she knows all their notes,
75 That gentle Maid! and oft, a moment's space,
What time the moon was lost behind a cloud,
Hath heard a pause of silence: till the Moon
Emerging, hath awaken'd earth and sky
With one sensation, and those wakeful Birds
80 Have all burst forth in choral minstrelsy,
As if one quick and sudden Gale had swept
An hundred airy harps! And she hath watch'd
Many a Nightingale perch giddily
On blosmy twig still swinging from the breeze,
85 And to that motion tune his wanton song,
Like tipsy Joy that reels with tossing head.

Farewell, O Warbler! till to-morrow eve,
And you, my friends! farewell, a short farewell!
We have been loitering long and pleasantly,
90 And now for our dear homes. – That strain again!

91   *my dear babe* – Hartley Coleridge, born in 1796.

What is Coleridge wishing for his son?

The Female Vagrant

Wordsworth redrafted this poem constantly and in its final form it was published in 1842 as part of a longer poem. This early version was written in 1793-4, 'partly to expose the vices of the penal law and the calamities of war as they affect individuals' (Wordsworth).

The narrative describes the female vagrant's life, beginning with her childhood, living harmoniously in the Lake District with her father, a farmer and fisherman. A new landowner ruins them by forfeiture of their fishing rights. The woman marries her childhood sweetheart, who has sought work in the city. Urban poverty forces the family to America. Caught up in the American War, she loses her soldier husband and her children to 'sword' and 'plague'. She returns to England, finding refuge for a while with gypsies, but, unable to accept robbery as a way of life, she becomes again an isolated wanderer. In her deep sorrow, she particularly mourns the loss of her 'inner self', the 'clear and open soul' she had as a child.

8   *fleecy store* – sheep (an example of the sort of eighteenth-century poetic diction that Wordsworth was rejecting).

Full fain it would delay me! – My dear Babe,
Who, capable of no articulate sound,
Mars all things with his imitative lisp,
How he would place his hand beside his ear,
His little hand, the small forefinger up,
And bid us listen! And I deem it wise
To make him Nature's playmate. He knows well
The evening star: and once when he awoke
In most distressful mood (some inward pain
Had made up that strange thing, an infant's dream)
I hurried with him to our orchard plot,
And he beholds the moon, and hush'd at once
Suspends his sobs, and laughs most silently,
While his fair eyes that swam with undropt tears
Did glitter in the yellow moon-beam! Well –
It is a father's tale. But if that Heaven
Should give me life, his childhood shall grow up
Familiar with these songs, that with the night
He may associate Joy! Once more farewell,
Sweet Nightingale! once more, my friends! farewell.

95

100

105

110

The Female Vagrant

By Derwent's side my Father's cottage stood,
(The Woman thus her artless story told)
One field, a flock, and what the neighbouring flood
Supplied, to him were more than mines of gold.
Light was my sleep; my days in transport roll'd:
With thoughtless joy I stretch'd along the shore
My father's nets, or watched, when from the fold
High o'er the cliffs I led my fleecy store,
A dizzy depth below! his boat and twinkling oar.

5

23 *gambols and wild freaks* – boisterous games.

34 *check'd* – restrained.

In the first four stanzas, Wordsworth emphasizes the sort of childhood the woman has had. Describe it in your own words.

40 *owned its sway* – acknowledged its power over them.

10 My father was a good and pious man,
   An honest man by honest parents bred,
   And I believe that, soon as I began
   To lisp, he made me kneel beside my bed,
   And in his hearing there my prayers I said:
15 And afterwards, by my good father taught,
   I read, and loved the books in which I read;
   For books in every neighbouring house I sought,
   And nothing to my mind a sweeter pleasure brought.

   Can I forget what charms did once adorn
20 My garden, stored with pease, and mint, and thyme,
   And rose and lilly for the sabbath morn?
   The sabbath bells, and their delightful chime;
   The gambols and wild freaks at shearing time;
   My hen's rich nest through long grass scarce espied;
25 The cowslip-gathering at May's dewy prime;
   The swans, that, when I sought the water-side,
   From far to meet me came, spreading their snowy pride.

   The staff I yet remember which upbore
   The bending body of my active sire;
30 His seat beneath the honeyed sycamore
   When the bees hummed, and chair by winter fire;
   When market-morning came, the neat attire
   With which, though bent on haste, myself I deck'd;
   My watchful dog, whose starts of furious ire,
35 When stranger passed, so often I have check'd;
   The red-breast known for years, which at my casement peck'd.

   The suns of twenty summers danced along, –
   Ah! little marked, how fast they rolled away:
   Then rose a mansion proud our woods among,
40 And cottage after cottage owned its sway,
   No joy to see a neighbouring house, or stray
   Through pastures not his own, the master took;

45 *brook* – endure.

46 *proffered gold* – inducement, pay-off.

What social injustices is Wordsworth exposing in lines 39–63 and 82–99?

My Father dared his greedy wish gainsay;
He loved his old hereditary nook,
45 And ill could I the thought of such sad parting brook.

But, when he had refused the proffered gold,
To cruel injuries he became a prey,
Sore traversed in whate'er he bought and sold.
His troubles grew upon him day by day,
50 Till all his substance fell into decay.
His little range of water was denied, *
All but the bed where his old body lay,
All, all was seized, and weeping, side by side,
We sought a home where we uninjured might abide.

55 Can I forget that miserable hour,
When from the last hill-top, my sire surveyed,
Peering above the trees, the steeple tower,
That on his marriage-day sweet music made!
Till then he hoped his bones might there be laid,
60 Close by my mother in their native bowers:
Bidding me trust in God, he stood and prayed, –
I could not pray: – through tears that fell in showers,
Glimmer'd our dear-loved home, alas! no longer ours!

There was a youth whom I had loved so long,
65 That when I loved him not I cannot say.
'Mid the green mountains many and many a song
We two had sung, like little birds in May.
When we began to tire of childish play
We seemed still more and more to prize each other:
70 We talked of marriage and our marriage day;
And I in truth did love him like a brother,
For never could I hope to meet with such another.

* Several of the Lakes in the north of England are let out to different Fishermen,
in parcels marked out by imaginary lines drawn from rock to rock.

74   *artist's* – artisan's. The 'empty loom' (line 89) implies a weaver.

93–4   These lines refer to the Army recruiting parade. Wives often followed
their soldier husbands.

His father said, that to a distant town
He must repair, to ply the artist's trade.
75 What tears of bitter grief till then unknown!
What tender vows our last sad kiss delayed!
To him we turned: – we had no other aid.
Like one revived, upon his neck I wept,
And her whom he had loved in joy, he said
80 He well could love in grief: his faith he kept;
And in a quiet home once more my father slept.

Four years each day with daily bread was blest,
By constant toil and constant prayer supplied.
Three lovely infants lay upon my breast;
85 And often, viewing their sweet smiles, I sighed,
And knew not why. My happy father died
When sad distress reduced the children's meal:
Thrice happy! that from him the grave did hide
The empty loom, cold hearth, and silent wheel,
90 And tears that flowed for ills which patience could not heal.

'Twas a hard change, an evil time was come;
We had no hope, and no relief could gain.
But soon, with proud parade, the noisy drum
Beat round, to sweep the streets of want and pain.
95 My husband's arms now only served to strain
Me and his children hungering in his view:
In such dismay my prayers and tears were vain:
To join those miserable men he flew;
And now to the sea-coast, with numbers more, we drew.

100 There foul neglect for months and months we bore,
Nor yet the crowded fleet its anchor stirred.
Green fields before us and our native shore,
By fever, from polluted air incurred,
Ravage was made, for which no knell was heard.
105 Fondly we wished, and wished away, nor knew,

110   *equinoctial deep* – the Atlantic around the time of the autumn equinox
      (21 September), when winds are high and seas rough.

116   *we the mercy of the waves should rue* – we should regret that we survived
      the voyage.

123–5   This hostile reference to the soldiers was omitted after 1800. (See
        Social and Political Background, page 210, for American War.)

'Mid that long sickness, and those hopes defer'd,
That happier days we never more must view:
The parting signal streamed, at last the land withdrew,

But from delay the summer calms were past.
110 On as we drove, the equinoctial deep
Ran mountains-high before the howling blast.
We gazed with terror on the gloomy sleep
Of them that perished in the whirlwind's sweep,
Untaught that soon such anguish must ensue,
115 Our hopes such harvest of affliction reap,
That we the mercy of the waves should rue.
We reached the western world, a poor, devoted crew.

Oh! dreadful price of being to resign
All that is dear *in* being! better far
120 In Want's most lonely cave till death to pine,
Unseen, unheard, unwatched by any star;
Or in the streets and walks where proud men are,
Better our dying bodies to obtrude,
Than dog-like, wading at the heels of war,
125 Protract a curst existence, with the brood
That lap (their very nourishment!) their brother's blood.

The pains and plagues that on our heads came down,
Disease and famine, agony and fear,
In wood or wilderness, in camp or town,
180 It would thy brain unsettle even to hear.
All perished – all, in one remorseless year,
Husband and children! one by one, by sword
And ravenous plague, all perished: every tear
Dried up, despairing, desolate, on board
135 A British ship I waked, as from a trance restored.

Peaceful as some immeasurable plain
By the first beams of dawning light impress'd,

150   *pallid* – pale.

What is the effect of the use of personification in lines 154–62?

163   *gulph* – gulf or chasm.

In the calm sunshine slept the glittering main.
The very ocean has its hour of rest,
140 That comes not to the human mourner's breast.
Remote from man, and storms of mortal care,
A heavenly silence did the waves invest;
I looked and looked along the silent air,
Until it seemed to bring a joy to my despair.

145 Ah! how unlike those late terrific sleeps!
And groans, that rage of racking famine spoke,
Where looks inhuman dwelt on festering heaps!
The breathing pestilence that rose like smoke!
The shriek that from the distant battle broke!
150 The mine's dire earthquake, and the pallid host
Driven by the bomb's incessant thunder-stroke
To loathsome vaults, where heart-sick anguish toss'd,
Hope died, and fear itself in agony was lost!

Yet does that burst of woe congeal my frame,
155 When the dark streets appeared to heave and gape,
While like a sea the storming army came,
And Fire from Hell reared his gigantic shape,
And Murder, by the ghastly gleam, and Rape
Seized their joint prey, the mother and the child!
160 But from these crazing thoughts my brain, escape!
– For weeks the balmy air breathed soft and mild,
And on the gliding vessel Heaven and Ocean smiled.

Some mighty gulph of separation past,
I seemed transported to another world: –
165 A thought resigned with pain, when from the mast
The impatient mariner the sail unfurl'd,
And whistling, called the wind that hardly curled
The silent sea. From the sweet thoughts of home,
And from all hope I was forever hurled.
170 For me – farthest from earthly port to roam

182 *cast on desart rock* – marooned on a desert island.

Was best, could I but shun the spot where man might come.

And oft, robb'd of my perfect mind, I thought
At last my feet a resting-place had found:
Here will I weep in peace, (so fancy wrought,)
175 Roaming the illimitable waters round;
Here watch, of every human friend disowned,
All day, my ready tomb the ocean-flood –
To break my dream the vessel reached its bound:
And homeless near a thousand homes I stood,
180 And near a thousand tables pined, and wanted food.

By grief enfeebled was I turned adrift,
Helpless as sailor cast on desart rock;
Nor morsel to my mouth that day did lift,
Nor dared my hand at any door to knock.
185 I lay, where with his drowsy mates, the cock
From the cross timber of an out-house hung;
How dismal tolled, that night, the city clock!
At morn my sick heart hunger scarcely stung,
Nor to the beggar's language could I frame my tongue.

190 So passed another day, and so the third:
Then did I try, in vain, the crowd's resort,
In deep despair by frightful wishes stirr'd,
Near the sea-side I reached a ruined fort:
There, pains which nature could no more support,
195 With blindness linked, did on my vitals fall;
Dizzy my brain, with interruption short
Of hideous sense; I sunk, nor step could crawl,
And thence was borne away to neighbouring hospital.

Recovery came with food: but still, my brain
200 Was weak, nor of the past had memory.
I heard my neighbours, in their beds, complain
Of many things which never troubled me;
Of feet still bustling round with busy glee,

214   *a faggot blazed* – a wood fire was burning.

215   *wild brood* – gypsies.

231   *boon* – cheerful, kind.

What is Wordsworth's attitude to the 'wild brood' (lines 215 et seq)?

Of looks where common kindness had no part,
205 Of service done with careless cruelty,
Fretting the fever round the languid heart,
And groans, which, as they said, would make a dead man start.

These things just served to stir the torpid sense,
Nor pain nor pity in my bosom raised.
210 Memory, though slow, returned with strength; and thence
Dismissed, again on open day I gazed,
At houses, men, and common light, amazed.
The lanes I sought, and as the sun retired,
Came, where beneath the trees a faggot blazed;
215 The wild brood saw me weep, my fate enquired,
And gave me food, and rest, more welcome, more desired.

My heart is touched to think that men like these,
The rude earth's tenants, were my first relief:
How kindly did they paint their vagrant ease!
220 And their long holiday that feared not grief,
For all belonged to all, and each was chief.
No plough their sinews strained; on grating road
No wain they drove, and yet, the yellow sheaf
In every vale for their delight was stowed:
225 For them, in nature's meads, the milky udder flowed.

Semblance, with straw and panniered ass, they made
Of potters wandering on from door to door:
But life of happier sort to me pourtrayed,
And other joys my fancy to allure;
230 The bag-pipe dinning on the midnight moor
In barn uplighted, and companions boon
Well met from far with revelry secure,
In depth of forest glade, when jocund June
Rolled fast along the sky his warm and genial moon.

258 *ruth* – pity, remorse.

Line 261 refers back to the beginning of the poem. Why?

235 But ill it suited me, in journey dark
O'er moor and mountain, midnight theft to hatch;
To charm the surly house-dog's faithful bark,
Or hang on tiptoe at the lifted latch;
The gloomy lantern, and the dim blue match,
240 The black disguise, the warning whistle shrill,
And ear still busy on its nightly watch,
Were not for me, brought up in nothing ill;
Besides, on griefs so fresh my thoughts were brooding still.

What could I do, unaided and unblest!
245 Poor Father! gone was every friend of thine:
And kindred of dead husband are at best
Small help, and, after marriage such as mine,
With little kindness would to me incline.
Ill was I then for toil or service fit:
250 With tears whose course no effort could confine,
By high-way side forgetful would I sit
Whole hours, my idle arms in moping sorrow knit.

I lived upon the mercy of the fields,
And oft of cruelty the sky accused;
255 On hazard, or what general bounty yields,
Now coldly given, now utterly refused.
The fields I for my bed have often used:
But, what afflicts my peace with keenest ruth
Is, that I have my inner self abused,
260 Foregone the home delight of constant truth,
And clear and open soul, so prized in fearless youth.

Three years a wanderer, often have I view'd,
In tears, the sun towards that country tend
Where my poor heart lost all its fortitude:
265 And now across this moor my steps I bend –
Oh! tell me whither – for no earthly friend
Have I. – She ceased, and weeping turned away,

Goody Blake, and Harry Gill,
A True Story

Wordsworth wrote this in the spring of 1798, having borrowed the book from which the story is taken (Erasmus Darwin, *Zoonomia* 1796) early in March. He asserts both in the Advertisement and the text that the story is true. It is obvious why it appealed to Wordsworth. Its subject is an old, poverty-stricken woman who, despite her hard work and general worthiness, cannot keep warm in winter. She is driven to an act of petty theft, much resented by the prosperous farmer whose hedges are depleted by her search for dry sticks. He leaves his warm fireside to waylay the thief, catching her in the act. Terrified, she curses him with cold. After that, whatever he does, he cannot keep warm.

21   *Auld* – old.

As if because her tale was at an end
She wept; – because she had no more to say
270 Of that perpetual weight which on her spirit lay.

Goody Blake, and Harry Gill,
A TRUE STORY

Oh! what's the matter? what's the matter?
What is't that ails young Harry Gill?
That evermore his teeth they chatter,
Chatter, chatter, chatter still.
5 Of waistcoats Harry has no lack,
Good duffle grey, and flannel fine;
He has a blanket on his back,
And coats enough to smother nine.

In March, December, and in July,
10 'Tis all the same with Harry Gill;
The neighbours tell, and tell you truly,
His teeth they chatter, chatter still.
At night, at morning, and at noon,
'Tis all the same with Harry Gill;
15 Beneath the sun, beneath the moon,
His teeth they chatter, chatter still.

Young Harry was a lusty drover,
And who so stout of limb as he?
His cheeks were red as ruddy clover,
20 His voice was like the voice of three.
Auld Goody Blake was old and poor,
Ill fed she was, and thinly clad;
And any man who pass'd her door,
Might see how poor a hut she had.

39 *canty* – lively and cheerful.
40 *linnet* – a songbird.

50 *rout* – noisy disturbance.

25   All day she spun in her poor dwelling,
      And then her three hours' work at night!
      Alas! 'twas hardly worth the telling,
      It would not pay for candle-light.
      – This woman dwelt in Dorsetshire,
30   Her hut was on a cold hill-side,
      And in that country coals are dear,
      For they come far by wind and tide.

      By the same fire to boil their pottage,
      Two poor old dames, as I have known,
35   Will often live in one small cottage,
      But she, poor woman, dwelt alone.
      'Twas well enough when summer came,
      The long, warm, lightsome summer-day,
      Then at her door the *canty* dame
40   Would sit, as any linnet gay.

      But when the ice our streams did fetter,
      Oh! then how her old bones would shake!
      You would have said, if you had met her,
      'Twas a hard time for Goody Blake.
45   Her evenings then were dull and dead;
      Sad case it was, as you may think,
      For very cold to go to bed,
      And then for cold not sleep a wink.

      Oh joy for her! when e'er in winter
50   The winds at night had made a rout,
      And scatter'd many a lusty splinter,
      And many a rotten bough about.
      Yet never had she, well or sick,
      As every man who knew her says,
55   A pile before-hand, wood or stick,
      Enough to warm her for three days.

73 *rick* – a stack of hay or straw, usually covered or thatched.

86 *bye-road* – or byroad, a secondary road or lane.

Now, when the frost was past enduring,
And made her poor old bones to ache,
Could any thing be more alluring,
60   Than an old hedge to Goody Blake?
And now and then, it must be said,
When her old bones were cold and chill,
She left her fire, or left her bed,
To seek the hedge of Harry Gill.

65   Now Harry he had long suspected
This trespass of old Goody Blake,
And vow'd that she should be detected,
And he on her would vengeance take.
And oft from his warm fire he'd go,
70   And to the fields his road would take,
And there, at night, in frost and snow,
He watch'd to seize old Goody Blake.

And once, behind a rick of barley,
Thus looking out did Harry stand;
75   The moon was full and shining clearly,
And crisp with frost the stubble-land.
– He hears a noise – he's all awake –
Again? – on tip-toe down the hill
He softly creeps – 'Tis Goody Blake,
80   She's at the hedge of Harry Gill.

Right glad was he when he beheld her:
Stick after stick did Goody pull,
He stood behind a bush of elder,
Till she had filled her apron full.
85   When with her load she turned about,
The bye-road back again to take,
He started forward with a shout,
And sprang upon poor Goody Blake.

How does Wordsworth present Goody Blake? Is she victim, villain, witch? Or something else?

Where is blame placed in the poem? (Be careful not to be too simplistic here).

Discuss the opposition of warm and cold in the poem.

What quality does Harry Gill show by responding to the curse in the way he does?

Why does Wordsworth twice repeat that the story is true? Why is it more valuable if true?

And fiercely by the arm he took her,
90 And by the arm he held her fast,
And fiercely by the arm he shook her,
And cried, "I've caught you then at last!"
Then Goody, who had nothing said,
Her bundle from her lap let fall;
95 And kneeling on the sticks, she pray'd
To God that is the judge of all.

She pray'd, her wither'd hand uprearing,
While Harry held her by the arm –
"God! who art never out of hearing,
100 "O may he never more be warm!"
The cold, cold moon above her head,
Thus on her knees did Goody pray,
Young Harry heard what she had said,
And icy-cold he turned away.

105 He went complaining all the morrow
That he was cold and very chill:
His face was gloom, his heart was sorrow,
Alas! that day for Harry Gill!
That day he wore a riding-coat,
110 But not a whit the warmer he:
Another was on Thursday brought,
And ere the Sabbath he had three.

'Twas all in vain, a useless matter,
And blankets were about him pinn'd;
115 Yet still his jaws and teeth they clatter,
Like a loose casement in the wind.
And Harry's flesh it fell away;
And all who see him say 'tis plain,
That, live as long as live he may,
120 He never will be warm again.

Lines
written at a small distance from my House,
and sent by my little Boy to the
Person to whom they are
addressed

Wordsworth wrote this lyric between March and May 1798. It is a direct address to Dorothy. The house is Alfoxden. The 'little boy' is the son of his friend Basil Montagu. William and Dorothy were looking after him at this time. See also *Anecdote for Fathers*. The specificity of the title reflects the concern for the specifics of time and place in the poem.

No word to any man he utters,
A bed or up, to young or old;
But ever to himself he mutters,
"Poor Harry Gill is very cold."
125 A-bed or up, by night or day;
His teeth they chatter, chatter still.
Now think, ye farmers all, I pray,
  Of Goody Blake and Harry Gill.

Lines

written at a small distance from my House, and sent by my little Boy to the Person to whom they are addressed

It is the first mild day of March:
Each minute sweeter than before,
The red-breast sings from the tall larch
That stands beside our door.

5 There is a blessing in the air,
Which seems a sense of joy to yield
To the bare trees, and mountains bare,
And grass in the green field.

My Sister! ('tis a wish of mine)
10 Now that our morning meal is done,
Make haste, your morning task resign;
Come forth and feel the sun.

13 *Edward* – the name given by Wordsworth to the 'little boy' (whose name, like his father's, was in fact Basil).

Why is this occasion memorable?

What mood is created?

What does 'living Calendar' (line 18) mean?

Why does 'Love' steal from 'heart to heart' (lines 21–4)?

Edward will come with you, and pray,
Put on with speed your woodland dress,
15 And bring no book, for this one day
We'll give to idleness.

No joyless forms shall regulate
Our living Calendar:
We from to-day, my friend, will date
20 The opening of the year.

Love, now an universal birth,
From heart to heart is stealing,
From earth to man, from man to earth,
– It is the hour of feeling.

25 One moment now may give us more
Than fifty years of reason;
Our minds shall drink at every pore
The spirit of the season.

Some silent laws our hearts may make,
30 Which they shall long obey;
We for the year to come may take
Our temper from to-day.

And from the blessed power that rolls
About, below, above;
35 We'll frame the measure of our souls,
They shall be tuned to love.

Then come, my sister! come, I pray,
With speed put on your woodland dress,
And bring no book; for this one day
40 We'll give to idleness.

Simon Lee
the Old Huntsman, with an incident
in which he was concerned

Wordsworth wrote this between March and May 1798. In the 1800 Preface he said that his intention was to put the reader 'in the way of receiving from ordinary moral sensations another and more salutary impression than we are accustomed to receive from them'.

1 *Cardigan* – the old man had, in fact, been huntsman to the squires of Alfoxden.

Simon Lee,
the Old Huntsman, with an incident
in which he was concerned

In the sweet shire of Cardigan,
Not far from pleasant Ivor-hall,
An old man dwells, a little man,
I've heard he once was tall.
5 Of years he has upon his back,
No doubt, a burthen weighty;
He says he is three score and ten,
But others say he's eighty.

A long blue livery-coat has he,
10 That's fair behind, and fair before;
Yet, meet him where you will, you see
At once that he is poor.
Full five and twenty years he lived
A running huntsman merry;
15 And, though he has but one eye left,
His cheek is like a cherry.

No man like him the horn could sound,
And no man was so full of glee;
To say the least, four counties round
20 Had heard of Simon Lee;
His master's dead, and no one now
Dwells in the hall of Ivor;
Men, dogs, and horses, all are dead;
He is the sole survivor.

25 His hunting feats have him bereft
Of his right eye, as you may see:
And then, what limbs those feats have left

47   *chiming hounds* – this refers to the cries of the hunting dogs.

Show how Wordsworth ensures that the reader is very aware of the contrast between Simon's youth and his old age.

To poor old Simon Lee!
He has no son, he has no child,
His wife, an aged woman,
Lives with him, near the waterfall,
Upon the village common.

And he is lean and he is sick,
His little body's half awry
His ancles they are swoln and thick
His legs are thin and dry.
When he was young he little knew
Of husbandry or tillage;
And now he's forced to work, though weak,
– The weakest in the village

He all the country could outrun,
Could leave both man and horse behind;
And often, ere the race was done,
He reeled and was stone-blind.
And still there's something in the world
At which his heart rejoices;
For when the chiming hounds are out,
He dearly loves their voices!

Old Ruth works out of doors with him,
And does what Simon cannot do;
For she, not over stout of limb,
Is stouter of the two.
And though you with your utmost skill
From labour could not wean them,
Alas! 'tis very little, all
Which they can do between them.

Beside their moss-grown hut of clay,
Not twenty paces from the door,
A scrap of land they have, but they

61–2   In the eighteenth century many thousands of acres of common land were
        enclosed.

64   *till* – cultivate (it).

What do you understand by lines 73–6?

*Explore all the associations that the old stump suggests. How effective is it as
a symbol in the poem?*

60   Are poorest of the poor.
      This scrap of land he from the heath
      Enclosed when he was stronger;
      But what avails the land to them,
      Which they can till no longer?

65   Few months of life has he in store,
      As he to you will tell,
      For still, the more he works, the more
      His poor old ancles swell.
      My gentle reader, I perceive
70   How patiently you've waited,
      And I'm afraid that you expect
      Some tale will be related.

      O reader! had you in your mind
      Such stores as silent thought can bring,
75   O gentle reader! you would find
      A tale in every thing.
      What more I have to say is short,
      I hope you'll kindly take it;
      It is no tale; but should you think,
80   Perhaps a tale you'll make it.

      One summer-day I chanced to see
      This old man doing all he could
      About the root of an old tree,
      A stump of rotten wood.
85   The mattock totter'd in his hand
      So vain was his endeavour
      That at the root of the old tree
      He might have worked for ever.

      "You're overtasked, good Simon Lee,
90   Give me your tool" to him I said;
      And at the word right gladly he

Anecdote for Fathers,
shewing how the art of lying may be taught

Wordsworth wrote this between March and May 1798. The child is Basil
Montagu's son, Basil or 'Edward' (see *Lines written at a small distance ...*, page
89). William and Dorothy became very fond of the boy, who reminded
William of his own childhood. Wordsworth uses the simple ballad-like poem
to subvert the didactic pieces of his contemporaries. Here it is the child who
is ultimately the teacher and the adult who is corrected.

Received my proffer'd aid.
I struck, and with a single blow
The tangled root I sever'd,
95 At which the poor old man so long
And vainly had endeavour'd.

The tears into his eyes were brought,
And thanks and praises seemed to run
So fast out of his heart, I thought
100 They never would have done.
– I've heard of hearts unkind, kind deeds
With coldness still returning.
Alas! the gratitude of men
Has oftner left me mourning.

Anecdote for Fathers,
shewing how the art of lying may be taught

I have a boy of five years old,
His face is fair and fresh to see;
His limbs are cast in beauty's mould,
And dearly he loves me.

5 One morn we stroll'd on our dry walk,
Our quiet house all full in view,
And held such intermitted talk
As we are wont to do.

My thoughts on former pleasures ran;
10 I thought of Kilve's delightful shore,
My pleasant home, when spring began,
A long, long year before.

20   *in very idleness* – for the sake of making conversation.

A day it was when I could bear
To think, and think, and think again;
15 With so much happiness to spare,
I could not feel a pain.

My boy was by my side, so slim
And graceful in his rustic dress!
And oftentimes I talked to him,
20 In very idleness.

The young lambs ran a pretty race;
The morning sun shone bright and warm;
"Kilve," said I, "was a pleasant place,
"And so is Liswyn farm.

25 "My little boy, which like you more,"
I said and took him by the arm –
"Our home by Kilve's delightful shore,
"Or here at Liswyn farm?"

"And tell me, had you rather be,"
30 I said and held him by the arm,
"At Kilve's smooth shore by the green sea,
"Or here at Liswyn farm?

In careless mood he looked at me,
While still I held him by the arm,
35 And said, "At Kilve I'd rather be
"Than here at Liswyn farm."

"Now, little Edward, say why so;
My little Edward, tell me why;"
"I cannot tell, I do not know."
40 "Why this is strange," said I.

Discuss the persona of the speaker of the poem. (Don't assume that it is necessarily Wordsworth.) 'Persona' means mask. What characteristics does the speaker show in the poem? Describe the change in the last stanza.

Why would Edward rather be at Kilve than Liswyn?

What has the speaker learnt from Edward?

We are seven

Wordsworth wrote this poem in the spring of 1798. He drew upon his memories of his 1793 tour of Britain. He read the poem to Dorothy and Coleridge, asking for suggestions for a preliminary, explanatory stanza. Coleridge immediately produced the stanza beginning 'A simple child, dear brother Jem'. 'Jem' was a joking reference to a friend. Wordsworth dropped this in later editions, leaving the first line as merely 'A simple child'. Wordsworth also drew on his own feelings about death when he was a child. 'Nothing was more difficult for me in childhood than to admit the notion of death as a state applicable to my own being' (footnote to *Intimations of Immortality*).

"For, here are woods and green-hills warm;
"There surely must some reason be
"Why you would change sweet Liswyn farm
"For Kilve by the green sea."

45 At this, my boy, so fair and slim,
Hung down his head, nor made reply;
And five times did I say to him,
"Why? Edward, tell me why?"

His head he raised – there was in sight,
50 It caught his eye, he saw it plain –
Upon the house-top, glittering bright,
A broad and gilded vane.

Then did the boy his tongue unlock,
And thus to me he made reply;
55 "At Kilve there was no weather-cock,
"And that's the reason why."

Oh dearest, dearest boy! my heart
For better lore would seldom yearn,
Could I but teach the hundredth part
60 Of what from thee I learn.

We are seven

A simple child, dear brother Jim,
That lightly draws its breath,
And feels its life in every limb,
What should it know of death?

Look at the characteristics of the speaker. Compare with the speaker in Anecdote for Fathers.

5   I met a little cottage girl,
    She was eight years old, she said;
    Her hair was thick with many a curl
    That cluster'd round her head.

    She had a rustic, woodland air,
10 And she was wildly clad;
    Her eyes were fair, and very fair,
    – Her beauty made me glad.

    "Sisters and brothers, little maid,
    "How many may you be?"
15 "How many? seven in all," she said,
    And wondering looked at me.

    "And where are they, I pray you tell?"
    She answered, "Seven are we,
    "And two of us at Conway dwell,
20 "And two are gone to sea.

    "Two of us in the church-yard lie,
    "My sister and my brother,
    "And in the church-yard cottage, I
    "Dwell near them with my mother."

25 "You say that two at Conway dwell,
    "And two are gone to sea,
    "Yet you are seven; I pray you tell
    "Sweet Maid, how this may be?"

    Then did the little Maid reply,
30 "Seven boys and girls are we;
    "Two of us in the church-yard lie,
    "Beneath the church-yard tree."

Contrast the two children in We are seven *and* Anecdote for Fathers.

"You run about, my little maid,
"Your limbs they are alive;
35   "If two are in the church-yard laid,
"Then ye are only five."

"Their graves are green, they may be seen,"
The little Maid replied,
"Twelve steps or more from my mother's door,
40   "And they are side by side.

"My stockings there I often knit,
"My 'kerchief there I hem;
"And there upon the ground I sit –
"I sit and sing to them.

45   "And often after sunset, Sir,
"When it is light and fair,
"I take my little porringer,
"And eat my supper there.

"The first that died was little Jane;
50   "In bed she moaning lay,
"Till God released her of her pain,
"And then she went away.

"So in the church-yard she was laid,
"And all the summer dry,
55   "Together round her grave we played,
"My brother John and I.

"And when the ground was white with snow,
"And I could run and slide,
"My brother John was forced to go,
60   "And he lies by her side."

Lines
written in early Spring

Another Wordsworth poem from the spring of 1798. It can be grouped with *Lines written at a small distance*, *Expostulation and Reply* and *The Tables Turned*.

He composed it in the 'grove' he mentioned – a shady spot near a waterfall.

"How many are you then," said I,
"If they two are in Heaven?"
The little Maiden did reply,
"O Master! we are seven."

65 "But they are dead; those two are dead!
"Their spirits are in heaven!"
"Twas throwing words away; for still
The little Maid would have her will,
And said, "Nay, we are seven!"

Lines
written in early spring

I heard a thousand blended notes,
While in a grove I sate reclined,
In that sweet mood when pleasant thoughts
Bring sad thoughts to the mind.

5 To her fair works did nature link
The human soul that through me ran;
And much it griev'd my heart to think
What man has made of man.

Through primrose-tufts, in that sweet bower,
10 The periwinkle trail'd its wreathes;
And 'tis my faith that every flower
Enjoys the air it breathes.

The birds around me hopp'd and play'd:
Their thoughts I cannot measure,
15 But the least motion which they made,
It seem'd a thrill of pleasure.

> *From the evidence of this volume of poetry, what has 'man made of man'?*

The Thorn

Wordsworth wrote this between March and May 1798. 'Arose out of my observing, on the ridge of Quantock Hill, on a stormy day, a thorn which I had often passed in calm and bright weather without noticing it. I said to myself, "Cannot I by some invention do as much to make this thorn permanently an impressive object as the storm has made it to my eyes at this moment?" I began the poem accordingly, and composed it with great rapidity ....' (Wordsworth to Isabella Fenwick, 1843).

There are some literary sources, in particular a Scottish ballad. The deserted woman, particularly as a mother, is a common theme in late eighteenth-century poetry. Wordsworth mentions this poem in the Advertisement, warning the reader that the narrator should not be taken to be the poet, but a 'loquacious' character who turns out to be a superstitious, rambling old seaman.

He tells the story of a young woman, jilted by her lover, and sent temporarily mad. It is rumoured that she gave birth to a child and subsequently killed it, and that her repeated visits to the thorn tree on the mountain are due to remorseful obsession. The rumour also states that, when men attempted to dig for the child's body there, the ground quivered and shook.

The budding twigs spread out their fan,
To catch the breezy air;
And I must think, do all I can,
20 That there was pleasure there.

If I these thoughts may not prevent,
If such be of my creed the plan,
Have I not reason to lament
What man has made of man!

The Thorn

I

There is a thorn; it looks so old,
In truth you'd find it hard to say,
How it could ever have been young,
It looks so old and grey.
5 Not higher than a two-years' child,
It stands erect this aged thorn;
No leaves it has, no thorny points;
It is a mass of knotted joints,
A wretched thing forlorn.
10 It stands erect, and like a stone
With lichens it is overgrown.

II

Like rock or stone, it is o'ergrown
With lichens to the very top,
And hung with heavy tufts of moss,
15 A melancholy crop:
Up from the earth these mosses creep,
And this poor thorn they clasp it round
So close, you'd say that they were bent
With plain and manifest intent,
20 To drag it to the ground;

32–3 *I've measured it from side to side 'Tis three feet long and two feet wide* – this couplet has attracted vituperative criticism for its naïve bathos ever since it was published, and has been widely parodied. It should be emphasized that Wordsworth is using a persona as a narrator, and these lines must be taken as an example of the narrator's limitations and his characteristic tone. However, it should perhaps be mentioned that Wordsworth's 'prosaic' language has lent itself to some interesting parodies, for example by Lewis Carroll. J.K. Stephen's parody of a Wordsworthian sonnet is worth reading as criticism as well as pastiche. (There are several parodies of Wordsworth, including this one, in E.O. Parrott's *Imitations of Immortality*, Penguin 1987.)

Paradoxically, writing a parody is one of the best ways to understand a writer's work, as it involves a thorough grasp of his or her stylistic characteristics. Try it on *We are seven*.

And all had joined in one endeavour
To bury this poor thorn for ever.

III

High on a mountain's highest ridge,
Where oft the stormy winter gale
25 Cuts like a scythe, while through the clouds
It sweeps from vale to vale;
Not five yards from the mountain-path,
This thorn you on your left espy;
And to the left, three yards beyond,
30 You see a little muddy pond
Of water, never dry;
I've measured it from side to side:
'Tis three feet long, and two feet wide.

IV

And close beside this aged thorn,
35 There is a fresh and lovely sight,
A beauteous heap, a hill of moss,
Just half a foot in height.
All lovely colours there you see,
All colours that were ever seen,
40 And mossy network too is there,
As if by hand of lady fair
The work had woven been,
And cups, the darlings of the eye
So deep is their vermilion dye.

V

45 Ah me! what lovely tints are there!
Of olive-green and scarlet bright,
In spikes, in branches, and in stars,
Green, red, and pearly white.
This heap of earth o'ergrown with moss
50 Which close beside the thorn you see,

Look back very carefully at lines 5, 17, 27, 32-3, 37, 41, 43, 52–5. The imagery suggests two quite specific references. One is obviously to measurement, and this further develops the narrator's character as pedantic and literal-minded. What is the other reference? Why is it placed at this point in the poem?

So fresh in all its beauteous dyes,
Is like an infant's grave in size
As like as like can be:
But never, never any where,
55 An infant's grave was half so fair.

VI

Now would you see this aged thorn,
This pond and beauteous hill of moss,
You must take care and chuse your time
The mountain when to cross.
60 For oft there sits, between the heap
That's like an infant's grave in size,
And that same pond of which I spoke,
A woman in a scarlet cloak,
And to herself she cries,
65 "Oh misery! oh misery!
"Oh woe is me! oh misery!"

VII

At all times of the day and night
This wretched woman thither goes,
And she is known to every star,
70 And every wind that blows;
And there beside the thorn she sits
When the blue day-light's in the skies,
And when the whirlwind's on the hill,
Or frosty air is keen and still,
75 And to herself she cries,
"Oh misery! oh misery!
"Oh woe is me! oh misery!"

VIII

"Now wherefore thus, by day and night,
"In rain, in tempest, and in snow,
80 "Thus to the dreary mountain-top

88 *doleful* – mournful, filled with sorrow.

"Does this poor woman go?
"And why sits she beside the thorn
"When the blue day-light's in the sky,
"Or when the whirlwind's on the hill,
85 "Or frosty air is keen and still,
"And wherefore does she cry? –
"Oh wherefore? wherefore? tell me why
"Does she repeat that doleful cry?"

IX

I cannot tell; I wish I could;
90 For the true reason no one knows,
But if you'd gladly view the spot,
The spot to which she goes;
The heap that's like an infant's grave,
The pond – and thorn, so old and grey,
95 Pass by her door – 'tis seldom shut –
And if you see her in her hut,
Then to the spot away! –
I never heard of such as dare
Approach the spot when she is there.

X

100 "But wherefore to the mountain-top
"Can this unhappy woman go,
"Whatever star is in the skies,
"Whatever wind may blow?"
Nay rack your brain – 'tis all in vain,
105 I'll tell you every thing I know;
But to the thorn, and to the pond
Which is a little step beyond,
I wish that you would go:
Perhaps when you are at the place
110 You something of her tale may trace.

119   *blithe* – carefree.

XI

I'll give you the best help I can:
Before you up the mountain go,
Up to the dreary mountain-top,
I'll tell you all I know.
115 'Tis now some two and twenty years,
Since she (her name is Martha Ray)
Gave with a maiden's true good will
Her company to Stephen Hill;
And she was blithe and gay,
120 And she was happy, happy still
Whene'er she thought of Stephen Hill.

XII

And they had fix'd the wedding-day,
The morning that must wed them both;
But Stephen to another maid
125 Had sworn another oath;
And with this other maid to church
Unthinking Stephen went –
Poor Martha! on that woful day
A cruel, cruel fire, they say,
130 Into her bones was sent:
It dried her body like a cinder,
And almost turn'd her brain to tinder.

XIII

They say, full six months after this,
While yet the summer-leaves were green,
135 She to the mountain-top would go,
And there was often seen.
'Tis said, a child was in her womb,
As now to any eye was plain;
She was with child, and she was mad,
140 Yet often she was sober sad
From her exceeding pain.

150   *wrought* – reached (for a similar idea, see *The Mad Mother*, lines 33–8).

Oh me! ten thousand times I'd rather
That he had died, that cruel father!

XIV

    Sad case for such a brain to hold
145 Communion with a stirring child!
    Sad case, as you may think, for one
    Who had a brain so wild!
    Last Christmas when we talked of this,
    Old Farmer Simpson did maintain,
150 That in her womb the infant wrought
    About its mother's heart, and brought
    Her senses back again:
    And when at last her time drew near,
    Her looks were calm, her senses clear.

XV

155 No more I know, I wish I did,
    And I would tell it all to you;
    For what became of this poor child
    There's none that ever knew:
    And if a child was born or no,
160 There's no one that could ever tell;
    And if 'twas born alive or dead,
    There's no one knows, as I have said,
    But some remember well,
    That Martha Ray about this time
165 Would up the mountain often climb.

XVI

    And all that winter, when at night
    The wind blew from the mountain-peak,
    'Twas worth your while, though in the dark,
    The church-yard path to seek:
170 For many a time and oft were heard
    Cries coming from the mountain-head,

176 *had to do with* – were connected with.

Some plainly living voices were,
And others, I've heard many swear,
Were voices of the dead:
175 I cannot think, whate'er they say,
They had to do with Martha Ray.

XVII

But that she goes to this old thorn,
The thorn which I've described to you,
And there sits in a scarlet cloak,
180 I will be sworn is true.
For one day with my telescope,
To view the ocean wide and bright,
When to this country first I came,
Ere I had heard of Martha's name,
185 I climbed the mountain's height:
A storm came on, and I could see
No object higher than my knee.

XVIII

'Twas mist and rain, and storm and rain,
No screen, no fence could I discover,
190 And then the wind! in faith, it was
A wind full ten times over.
I looked around, I thought I saw
A jutting crag, and off I ran,
Head-foremost, through the driving rain,
195 The shelter of the crag, to gain
And, as I am a man,
Instead of jutting crag, I found
A woman seated on the ground.

XIX

I did not speak – I saw her face,
200 Her face it was enough for me;
I turned about and heard her cry,

Martha Ray is described (stanza VI) as a 'woman in a scarlet cloak'. She is also described by her situation and location: she is 'placed' among the natural objects on the mountain – the thorn tree, the pond, the hill of moss. What effect does this have? Look particularly at stanza XVIII.

"O misery! O misery!"
And there she sits, until the moon
Through half the clear blue sky will go,
205 And when the little breezes make
The waters of the pond to shake,
As all the country know,
She shudders and you hear her cry,
"Oh misery! oh misery!

XX

210 "But what's the thorn? and what's the pond?
"And what's the hill of moss to her?
"And what's the creeping breeze that comes
"The little pond to stir?"
I cannot tell; but some will say
215 She hanged her baby on the tree,
Some say she drowned it in the pond,
Which is a little step beyond,
But all and each agree,
The little babe was buried there,
220 Beneath that hill of moss so fair.

I've heard the scarlet moss is red
With drops of that poor infant's blood;
But kill a new-born infant thus!
I do not think she could.
225 Some say, if to the pond you go,
And fix on it a steady view,
The shadow of a babe you trace,
A baby and a baby's face,
And that it looks at you;
230 Whene'er you look on it, 'tis plain
The baby looks at you again.

> *Describe the characteristics of the narrator. How do these affect the way he tells the story?*

> *Is the narrator making any judgement of Martha Ray? What is his attitude to her?*

The Last of the Flock

Wordsworth wrote this in the creative burst of March–May 1798. It is based on a local incident, but has more general application. On the surface, Wordsworth is attacking the system of parish relief which withholds benefits from a poor man while he still has some property (lines 41–50). He is also attacking the belief that property is a cause of evil and source of misery to the poor. Wordsworth is here rejecting the influence of Godwin (see **Cultural and Literary Background**, page 215) and moving away from his own younger, revolutionary self.

XXII

And some had sworn an oath that she
Should be to public justice brought;
And for the little infant's bones
235 With spades they would have sought.
But then the beauteous hill of moss
Before their eyes began to stir;
And for full fifty yards around,
The grass it shook upon the ground;
240 But all do still aver
The little babe is buried there,
Beneath that hill of moss so fair.

XXIII

I cannot tell how this may be,
But plain it is, the thorn is bound
245 With heavy tufts of moss, that strive
To drag it to the ground.
And this I know, full many a time,
When she was on the mountain high,
By day, and in the silent night,
250 When all the stars shone clear and bright,
That I have heard her cry,
"Oh misery! oh misery!
"O woe is me! oh misery!"

The Last of the Flock

In distant countries I have been,
And yet I have not often seen
A healthy man, a man full grown
Weep in the public roads alone.
5 But such a one, on English ground,
And in the broad high-way, I met;

What is the effect of having a listener – or frame narrator – meeting the shepherd on the road? How does it add to the poem?

13   *made essay* – attempted.

19   *rock* – mountain.

37   *lusty* – well-grown, healthy.

Along the broad high-way he came,
His cheeks with tears were wet.
Sturdy he seemed, though he was sad;
10 And in his arms a lamb he had.

He saw me, and he turned aside,
As if he wished himself to hide:
Then with his coat he made essay
To wipe those briny tears away.
15 I follow'd him, and said, "My friend
"What ails you? wherefore weep you so?"
– "Shame on me, Sir! this lusty lamb,
He makes my tears to flow.
To-day I fetched him from the rock;
20 He is the last of all my flock.

When I was young, a single man,
And after youthful follies ran,
Though little given to care and thought,
Yet, so it was, a ewe I bought;
25 And other sheep from her I raised,
As healthy sheep as you might see,
And then I married, and was rich
As I could wish to be;
Of sheep I number'd a full score,
30 And every year encreas'd my store.

Year after year my stock it grew,
And from this one, this single ewe,
Full fifty comely sheep I raised,
As sweet a flock as ever grazed!
35 Upon the mountain did they feed;
They throve, and we at home did thrive.
– This lusty lamb of all my store
Is all that is alive:
And now I care not if we die,
40 And perish all of poverty.

44 *I of the parish ask'd relief* – under the Elizabethan Poor Law (still operative, in modified form, in the eighteenth century), the parish was responsible for the relief of the destitute.

Ten children, Sir! had I to feed,
Hard labour in a time of need!
My pride was tamed, and in our grief
I of the parish ask'd relief.
45 They said I was a wealthy man;
My sheep upon the mountain fed,
And it was fit that thence I took
Whereof to buy us bread:"
"Do this; how can we give to you,"
50 They cried, "what to the poor is due?"

I sold a sheep as they had said,
And bought my little children bread,
And they were healthy with their food;
For me it never did me good.
55 A woeful time it was for me,
To see the end of all my gains,
The pretty flock which I had reared
With all my care and pains,
To see it melt like snow away!
60 For me it was a woeful day.
Another still! and still another!

A little lamb, and then its mother!
It was a vein that never stopp'd,
Like blood-drops from my heart they dropp'd.
65 Till thirty were not left alive
They dwindled, dwindled, one by one,
And I may say that many a time
I wished they all were gone:
They dwindled one by one away;
70 For me it was a woeful day.

93   *weather* – a castrated ram.

Why was the shepherd inclined to 'wicked deeds' (line 71)?

Look at lines 81–90. What is the shepherd saying? What has his love for his children to do with the size of his flock?

To wicked deeds I was inclined,
And wicked fancies cross'd my mind,
And every man I chanc'd to see,
I thought he knew some ill of me.
75 No peace, no comfort could I find,
No ease, within doors or without,
And crazily, and wearily,
I went my work about.
Oft-times I thought to run away;
80 For me it was a woeful day.

Sir! 'twas a precious flock to me,
As dear as my own children be;
For daily with my growing store
I loved my children more and more.
85 Alas! it was an evil time;
God cursed me in my sore distress,
I prayed, yet every day I thought
I loved my children less;
And every week, and every day,
90 My flock, it seemed to melt away.

They dwindled, Sir, sad sight to see!
From ten to five, from five to three,
A lamb, a weather, and a ewe;
And then at last, from three to two;
95 And of my fifty, yesterday
I had but only one,
And here it lies upon my arm,
Alas! and I have none;
To-day I fetched it from the rock
100 It is the last of all my flock."

The Dungeon

This poem is an extract from Coleridge's play *Osorio*, 1797 (see Note to *The Foster-Mother's Tale*, page 46). Penal reform and the treatment of prisoners was one of the preoccupations of the 1790s. (See Wordsworth's *The Convict*, page 91 and, in the Appendix, *On the Necessity of Solitary Confinement* and *A Prison*.)

Coleridge asks 'Is this the only cure?' (line 5). Describe Coleridge's suggested cure (lines 20–30).

The Dungeon

And this place our forefathers made for man!
This is the process of our love and wisdom,
To each poor brother who offends against us –
Most innocent, perhaps – and what if guilty?
5 Is this the only cure? Merciful God?
Each pore and natural outlet shrivell'd up
By ignorance and parching poverty,
His energies roll back upon his heart,
And stagnate and corrupt; till changed to poison,
10 They break out on him, like a loathsome plague-spot;
Then we call in our pamper'd mountebanks –
And this is their best cure! uncomforted
And friendless solitude, groaning and tears,
And savage faces, at the clanking hour,
15 Seen through the steams and vapour of his dungeon,
By the lamp's dismal twilight! So he lies
Circled with evil, till his very soul
Unmoulds its essence, hopelessly deformed
By sights of ever more deformity!

20 With other ministrations thou, O nature!
Healest thy wandering and distempered child:
Thou pourest on him thy soft influences,
Thy sunny hues, fair forms, and breathing sweets,
Thy melodies of woods, and winds, and waters,
25 Till he relent, and can no more endure
To be a jarring and a dissonant thing,
Amid this general dance and minstrelsy;
But, bursting into tears, wins back his way,
His angry spirit healed and harmonized
30 By the benignant touch of love and beauty.

The Mad Mother

Another Wordsworth poem from the Alfoxden spring of 1798. 'The subject was reported to me by a lady of Bristol who had seen the poor creature' (Wordsworth). There are similarities between this and *The Complaint of a Forsaken Indian Woman*, written at much the same time. Both poems deal with the emotion felt by a destitute and abandoned mother for her son.

4   *main* – sea.

10   *And it was in the English tongue* – Wordsworth suggested in 1836 'though she came from far, English was her native tongue – which shows her either to be of these Islands, or a North American'.

What has happened to the woman? Why is she mad? Describe the woman's relationship with her husband, looking at all the references to him.

What is the woman referring to when she talks about 'fiendish faces' that 'hung at my breast and pulled at me' (lines 23-4)?

The Mad Mother

Her eyes are wild, her head is bare,
The sun has burnt her coal-black hair,
Her eye-brows have a rusty stain,
And she came far from over the main.
5 She has a baby on her arm,
Or else she were alone;
And underneath the hay-stack warm,
And on the green-wood stone,
She talked and sung the woods among;
10 And it was in the English tongue.

"Sweet babe! they say that I am mad,
But nay, my heart is far too glad;
And I am happy when I sing
Full many a sad and doleful thing:
15 Then, lovely baby, do not fear!
I pray thee have no fear of me,
But, safe as in a cradle, here
My lovely baby! thou shalt be,
To thee I know too much I owe;
20 I cannot work thee any woe.

A fire was once within my brain;
And in my head a dull, dull pain;
And fiendish faces one, two, three,
Hung at my breasts , and pulled at me.
25 But then there came a sight of joy;
It came at once to do me good;
I waked, and saw my little boy,
My little boy of flesh and blood;
Oh joy for me that sight to see!
30 For he was here, and only he.

Describe the benefits the mother derives from the physical contact with her son.

Suck, little babe, oh suck again!
It cools my blood; it cools my brain;
Thy lips I feel them, baby! they
Draw from my heart the pain away.
35 Oh! press me with thy little hand;
It loosens something at my chest;
About that tight and deadly band
I feel thy little fingers press'd.
The breeze I see is in the tree;
40 It comes to cool my babe and me.

Oh! love me, love me, little boy!
Thou art thy mother's only joy;
And do not dread the waves below,
When o'er the sea-rock's edge we go;
45 The high crag cannot work me harm,
Nor leaping torrents when they howl;
The babe I carry on my arm,
He saves for me my precious soul;
Then happy lie, for blest am I;
50 Without me my sweet babe would die.

Then do not fear, my boy! for thee
Bold as a lion I will be;
And I will always be thy guide,
Through hollow snows and rivers wide
55 I'll build an Indian bower; I know
The leaves that make the softest bed:
And if from me thou wilt not go,
But still be true 'till I am dead,
My pretty thing! then thou shalt sing,
60 As merry as the birds in spring.

Thy father cares not for my breast,
'Tis thine, sweet baby, there to rest:
'Tis all thine own! and if its hue
Be changed, that was so fair to view,

74 *honesty* – simplicity.

> *How realistic are the mother's expectations about the future life she will lead with her son in the countryside?*

65 'Tis fair enough for thee, my dove!
My beauty, little child, is flown;
But thou wilt live with me in love,
And what if my poor cheek be brown?
'Tis well for me; thou canst not see
70 How pale and wan it else would be.

Dread not their taunts, my little life!
I am thy father's wedded wife;
And underneath the spreading tree
We two will live in honesty.
75 If his sweet boy he could forsake,
With me he never would have stay'd:
From him no harm my babe can take,
But he, poor man! is wretched made;
And every day we two will pray
80 For him that's gone and far away.

I'll teach my boy the sweetest things;
I'll teach him how the owlet sings.
My little babe! thy lips are still,
And thou hast almost suck'd thy fill.
85 — Where art thou gone my own dear child?
What wicked looks are those I see?
Alas! alas! that look so wild,
It never, never came from me:
If thou art mad, my pretty lad,
90 Then I must be for ever sad.

Oh! smile on me, my little lamb!
For I thy own dear mother am.
My love for thee has well been tried:
I've sought thy father far and wide.
95 I know the poisons of the shade,
I know the earth-nuts fit for food;

The Idiot Boy

'Alfoxden 1798. The last stanza – 'The Cock did crow to-whoo, to-whoo, And the sun did shine so cold' – was the foundation of the whole. The words were reported to me by my dear friend Thomas Poole, but I have since heard the same repeated of other Idiots. Let me add that this long poem was composed in the groves of Alfoxden almost extempore; not a word, I believe, being corrected, though one stanza was omitted. I mention this in gratitude to those happy moments, for in truth, I never wrote anything with so much glee.' (Wordsworth to Isabella Fenwick, 1843.)

The poem was harshly attacked by Southey in the **Critical Review**, October 1798 – 'No tale less deserved the labour that appears to have been bestowed on this.' Later attacks came, even from Coleridge. Wordsworth's response in 1802 to Wilson is worth quoting for the light it sheds on the poet's attitude to his readers.

> 'It is not enough for me as a Poet, to delineate merely such feelings as all men *do* sympathise with; but it is also highly desirable to add to these others, such as all men *may* sympathise with, and such as there is reason to believe they would be better and more moral beings if they did sympathise with....'
>
> (Letter to John Wilson, 1802)

The poem remained a favourite with Wordsworth.

Jot down your reactions to the poem as you are reading it. Do they include a range of differing feelings? Do you find yourself sympathizing with the feelings described in the poem?

What is the narrator's attitude to the Idiot Boy?

Then, pretty dear, be not afraid;
We'll find thy father in the wood.
Now laugh and be gay, to the woods away!
100   And there, my babe, we'll live for aye.

The Idiot Boy

'Tis eight o'clock, – a clear March night,
The moon is up – the sky is blue,
The owlet in the moonlight air,
He shouts from nobody knows where;
5   He lengthens out his lonely shout,
Halloo! halloo! a long halloo!

– Why bustle thus about your door,
What means this bustle, Betty Foy?
Why are you in this mighty fret?
10   And why on horseback have you set
Him whom you love, your idiot boy?

Beneath the moon that shines so bright,
Till she is tired, let Betty Foy
With girt and stirrup fiddle-faddle;
15   But wherefore set upon a saddle
Him who she loves, her idiot boy?

There's scarce a soul that's out of bed;
Good Betty! put him down again;
His lips with joy they burr at you,
20   But, Betty! what has he to do
With stirrup, saddle, or with rein?

The world will say 'tis very idle,
Bethink you of the time of night;
There's not a mother, no not one,

46   *faggots* – bundles of sticks for firewood.

52   *post* – ride.

25 But when she hears what you have done,
    Oh! Betty she'll be in a fright.

    But Betty's bent on her intent,
    For her good neighbour, Susan Gale,
    Old Susan, she who dwells alone,
30 Is sick, and makes a piteous moan,
    As if her very life would fail.

    There's not a house within a mile,
    No hand to help them in distress:
    Old Susan lies a bed in pain,
35 And sorely puzzled are the twain,
    For what she ails they cannot guess.
    And Betty's husband's at the wood,
    Where by the week he doth abide,
    A woodman in the distant vale;
40 There's none to help poor Susan Gale,
    What must be done? what will betide?

    And Betty from the lane has fetched
    Her pony, that is mild and good,
    Whether he be in joy or pain,
45 Feeding at will along the lane,
    Or bringing faggots from the wood.

    And he is all in travelling trim,
    And by the moonlight, Betty Foy
    Has up upon the saddle set,
50 The like was never heard of yet,
    Him whom she loves, her idiot boy.

    And he must post without delay
    Across the bridge that's in the dale,
    And by the church, and o'er the down,

60   *hurly-burly* – commotion, turbulence.

55 To bring a doctor from the town,
Or she will die, old Susan Gale.

There is no need of boot or spur,
There is no need of whip or wand,
For Johnny has his holly-bough,
60 And with a hurly-burly now
He shakes the green bough in his hand.

And Betty o'er and o'er has told
The boy who is her best delight,
Both what to follow, what to shun,
65 What do, and what to leave undone,
How turn to left, and how to right.

And Betty's most especial charge,
Was, "Johnny! Johnny! mind that you
"Come home again, nor stop at all,
70 "Come home again, whate'er befal,
"My Johnny do, I pray you do."

To this did Johnny answer make,
Both with his head, and with his hand,
And proudly shook the bridle too,
75 And then! his words were not a few,
Which Betty well could understand.

And now that Johnny is just going,
Though Betty's in a mighty flurry,
She gently pats the pony's side,
80 On which her idiot boy must ride,
And seems no longer in a hurry.

But when the pony moved his legs,
Oh! then for the poor idiot boy!

100   *trim* – order, readiness.

104   *guide-post* – signpost.

For joy he cannot hold the bridle,
85   For joy his head and heels are idle,
He's idle all for very joy.

And while the pony moves his legs,
In Johnny's left-hand you may see,
The green bough's motionless and dead;
90   The moon that shines above his head
Is not more still and mute than he.

His heart it was so full of glee,
That till fifty yards were gone,
He quite forgot his holly whip,
95   And all his skill in horsemanship,
Oh! happy, happy, happy John.

And Betty's standing at the door,
And Betty's face with joy o'erflows,
Proud of herself, and proud of him,
100   She sees him in his travelling trim;
How quietly her Johnny goes.

The silence of her idiot boy,
What hopes it sends to Betty's heart!
He's at the guide-post – he turns right,
105   She watches till he's out of sight,
And Betty will not then depart.

Burr, burr – now Johnny's lips they burr,
As loud as any mill, or near it,
Meek as a lamb the pony moves,
110   And Johnny makes the noise he loves,
And Betty listens, glad to hear it.

Away she hies to Susan Gale:
And Johnny's in a merry tune,

114 *curr* – an onomatopoeic word which represents the sound made by the owls. It seems to have been invented by Wordsworth, presumably for the sake of the rhyme here.

121 *out of humour* – ill-tempered.

139 *porringer* – bowl.

The owlets hoot, the owlets curr,
115 And Johnny's lips they burr, burr, burr,
And on he goes beneath the moon.

His steed and he right well agree,
For of this pony there's a rumour,
That should he lose his eyes and ears,
120 And should he live a thousand years,
He never will be out of humour.

But then he is a horse that thinks!
And when he thinks his pace is slack;
Now, though he knows poor Johnny well,
125 Yet for his life he cannot tell
What he has got upon his back.

So through the moonlight lanes they go,
And far into the moonlight dale,
And by the church, and o'er the down,
130 To bring a doctor from the town,
To comfort poor old Susan Gale.

And Betty, now at Susan's side,
Is in the middle of her story,
What comfort Johnny soon will bring,
135 With many a most diverting thing,
Of Johnny's wit and Johnny's glory.

And Betty's still at Susan's side:
By this time she's not quite so flurried;
Demure with porringer and plate
140 She sits, as if in Susan's fate
Her life and soul were buried.

But Betty, poor good woman! she,
You plainly in her face may read it,

168   *vile* – repulsive or disgusting, wretched or shameful.

Could lend out of that moment's store
145 Five years of happiness or more,
To any that might need it.

But yet I guess that now and then
With Betty all was not so well,
And to the road she turns her ears,
150 And thence full many a sound she hears,
Which she to Susan will not tell.

Poor Susan moans, poor Susan groans,
"As sure as there's a moon in heaven,"
Cries Betty, "he'll be back again;
155 "They'll both be here, 'tis almost ten,
"They'll both be here before eleven."

Poor Susan moans, poor Susan groans,
The clock gives warning for eleven;
'Tis on the stroke – "If Johnny's near,"
160 Quoth Betty "he will soon be here,
"As sure as there's a moon in heaven."

The clock is on the stroke of twelve,
And Johnny is not yet in sight,
The moon's in heaven, as Betty sees,
165 But Betty is not quite at ease;
And Susan has a dreadful night.

And Betty, half an hour ago,
On Johnny vile reflections cast;
"A little idle sauntering thing!"
170 With other names, an endless string,
But now that time is gone and past.

178   *quandary* – dilemma, state of indecision.

191   *rue* – regret.

And Betty's drooping at the heart,
That happy time all past and gone,
"How can it be he is so late?
175 "The doctor he has made him wait,
"Susan! they'll both be here anon."

And Susan's growing worse and worse,
And Betty's in a sad quandary;
And then there's nobody to say
180 If she must go or she must stay:
– She's in a sad quandary.

The clock is on the stroke of one;
But neither Doctor nor his guide
Appear along the moonlight road,
185 There's neither horse nor man abroad,
And Betty's still at Susan's side.

And Susan she begins to fear
Of sad mischances not a few,
That Johnny may perhaps be drown'd,
190 Or lost perhaps, and never found;
Which they must both for ever rue.

She prefaced half a hint of this
With, "God forbid it should be true!"
At the first word that Susan said
195 Cried Betty, rising from the bed,
"Susan, I'd gladly stay with you.

"I must be gone, I must away,
"Consider, Johnny's but half-wise;
"Susan, we must take care of him,
200 "If he is hurt in life or limb" –
"Oh God forbid!" poor Susan cries.

209 *hies* – goes, hurries.

"What can I do?" says Betty, going,
"What can I do to ease your pain?
"Good Susan tell me, and I'll stay;
205 "I fear you're in a dreadful way,
"But I shall soon be back again."

"Good Betty go, good Betty go,
"There's nothing that can ease my pain."
Then off she hies, but with a prayer
210 That God poor Susan's life would spare,
Till she comes back again.

So, through the moonlight lane she goes,
And far into the moonlight dale;
And how she ran, and how she walked,
215 And all that to herself she talked,
Would surely be a tedious tale.

In high and low, above, below,
In great and small, in round and square,
In tree and tower was Johnny seen,
220 In bush and brake, in black and green,
'Twas Johnny, Johnny, every where.

She's past the bridge that's in the dale,
And now the thought torments her sore,
Johnny perhaps his horse forsook,
225 To hunt the moon that's in the brook,
And never will be heard of more.

And now she's high upon the down,
Alone amid a prospect wide;
There's neither Johnny nor his horse,
230 Among the fern or in the gorse;
There's neither doctor nor his guide.

250   *cattle* – obsolete generic term for 'animals'.

"Oh saints! what is become of him!
"Perhaps he's climbed into an oak,
"Where he will stay till he is dead;
235 "Or sadly he has been misled,
"And joined the wandering gypsey-folk.

"Or him that wicked pony's carried
"To the dark cave, the goblins' hall,
"Or in the castle he's pursuing,
240 "Among the ghosts, his own undoing;
"Or playing with the waterfall."

At poor old Susan then she railed,
While to the town she posts away;
"If Susan had not been so ill,
245 "Alas! I should have had him still,
"My Johnny, till my dying day."

Poor Betty! in this sad distemper,
The doctor's self would hardly spare,
Unworthy things she talked and wild,
250 Even he, of cattle the most mild,
The pony had his share.

And now she's got into the town,
And to the doctor's door she hies;
'Tis silence all on every side;
255 The town so long, the town so wide,
Is silent as the skies.

And now she's at the doctor's door,
She lifts the knocker, rap, rap, rap,
The doctor at the casement shews,
260 His glimmering eyes that peep and doze;
And one hand rubs his old night-cap.

What is your reaction to Betty Foy? Do you agree with Coleridge that her 'folly' is equal to the 'idiocy' of her son? (See **Critical Approaches**, page 227.)

"Oh Doctor! Doctor! where's my Johnny?"
"I'm here, what is't you want with me?"
"Oh Sir! you know I'm Betty Foy,
265 "And I have lost my poor dear boy,
"You know him – him you often see;

"He's not so wise as some folks be."
"The devil take his wisdom!" said
The Doctor, looking somewhat grim,
270 "What, woman! should I know of him?"
And, grumbling, he went back to bed.

"O woe is me! O woe is me!
"Here will I die; here will I die;
"I thought to find my Johnny here,
275 "But he is neither far nor near,
"Oh! what a wretched mother I!"

She stops, she stands, she looks about,
Which way to turn she cannot tell.
Poor Betty! it would ease her pain
280 If she had heart to knock again;
– The clock strikes three – a dismal knell!

Then up along the town she hies,
No wonder if her senses fail,
This piteous news so much it shock'd her,
285 She quite forgot to send the Doctor,
To comfort poor old Susan Gale.

And now she's high upon the down,
And she can see a mile of road,
"Oh cruel! I'm almost three-score;
290 "Such night as this was ne'er before,
"There's not a single soul abroad."

299   *hob nob* – on familiar terms, close.

303   *deadly sin* – suicide (considered a mortal sin by the Church).

She listens, but she cannot hear
The foot of horse, the voice of man;
The streams with softest sound are flowing,
295 The grass you almost hear it growing,
You hear it now if e'er you can.

The owlets through the long blue night
Are shouting to each other still:
Fond lovers, yet not quite hob nob,
300 They lengthen out the tremulous sob,
That echoes far from hill to hill.

Poor Betty now has lost all hope,
Her thoughts are bent on deadly sin;
A green-grown pond she just has pass'd,
305 And from the brink she hurries fast,
Lest she should drown herself therein.

And now she sits her down and weeps;
Such tears she never shed before;
"Oh dear, dear pony! my sweet joy!
310 "Oh carry back my idiot boy!
"And we will ne'er o'erload thee more."

A thought is come into her head;
"The pony he is mild and good,
"And we have always used him well;
315 "Perhaps he's gone along the dell,
"And carried Johnny to the wood."

Then up she springs as if on wings;
She thinks no more of deadly sin;
If Betty fifty ponds should see,
320 The last of all her thoughts would be,
To drown herself therein.

341   *desart* – desert.

347   *the muses* – The Nine Muses were female figures supposed to give divine inspiration to creative artists, according to Greek myth.

348   *indentures* – Apprentices were indentured to their masters so that they could learn a trade or craft. The indentures were a form of contract. The contract would last for a number of years, but it rarely lasted fourteen. Wordsworth is being ironic about the length of time it takes to become a poet.

Oh reader! now that I might tell
What Johnny and his horse are doing
What they've been doing all this time,
325 Oh could I put it into rhyme,
A most delightful tale pursuing!

Perhaps and no unlikely thought!
He with his pony now doth roam
The cliffs and peaks so high that are,
330 To lay his hands upon a star,
And in his pocket bring it home.

Perhaps he's turned himself about,
His face unto his horse's tail,
And still and mute, in wonder lost,
335 All like a silent horseman-ghost,
He travels on along the vale.

And now, perhaps, he's hunting sheep,
A fierce and dreadful hunter he!
Yon valley, that's so trim and green,
340 In five months' time, should he be seen,
A desert wilderness will be.

Perhaps, with head and heels on fire,
And like the very soul of evil,
He's galloping away, away,
345 And so he'll gallop on for aye,
The bane of all that dread the devil.

I to the muses have been bound,
These fourteen years, by strong indentures;
Oh gentle muses! let me tell
350 But half of what to him befel,
For sure he met with strange adventures.

Why does the narrator draw attention to the fact that he is telling a story by asking the Muses for help (349–56) and then not getting any help? Is he drawing attention to the fact that he is a poet or is he suggesting something about the subject – that he can't know what the Idiot Boy was doing when he was by himself? Is the Boy unknowable?

Oh gentle muses! is this kind?
Why will ye thus my suit repel?
Why of your further aid bereave me?
355   And can ye thus unfriended leave me?
Ye muses! whom I love so well.

Who's yon, that, near the waterfall,
Which thunders down with headlong force,
Beneath the moon, yet shining fair,
360   As careless as if nothing were,
Sits upright on a feeding horse?

Unto his horse, that's feeding free,
He seems, I think, the rein to give;
Of moon or stars he takes no heed;
365   Of such we in romances read,
    – 'Tis Johnny! Johnny! as I live.

And that's the very pony too.
Where is she, where is Betty Foy?
She hardly can sustain her fears;
370   The roaring water-fall she hears,
And cannot find her idiot boy.

Your pony's worth his weight in gold,
Then calm your terrors, Betty Foy!
She's coming from among the trees,
375   And now, all full in view, she sees
Him whom she loves, her idiot boy.

And Betty sees the pony too:
Why stand you thus Good Betty Foy?
It is no goblin, 'tis no ghost,
380   'Tis he whom you so long have lost,
He whom you love, your idiot boy.

390   *quaffs* – drinks deeply.

She looks again — her arms are up –
She screams — she cannot move for joy;
She darts as with a torrent's force,
385 She almost has o'erturned the horse,
And fast she holds her idiot boy.

And Johnny burrs and laughs aloud,
Whether in cunning or in joy,
I cannot tell; but while he laughs,
390 Betty a drunken pleasure quaffs,
To hear again her idiot boy.

And now she's at the pony's tail,
And now she's at the pony's head,
On that side now, and now on this,
395 And almost stifled with her bliss,
A few sad tears does Betty shed.

She kisses o'er and o'er again,
Him whom she loves, her idiot boy,
She's happy here, she's happy there,
400 She is uneasy every where;
Her limbs are all alive with joy.

She pats the pony, where or when
She knows not, happy Betty Foy!
The little pony glad may be,
405 But he is milder far than she,
You hardly can perceive his joy.

"Oh! Johnny, never mind the Doctor;
"You've done your best, and that is all."
She took the reins, when this was said,
410 And gently turned the pony's head
From the loud water-fall.

Why and how does Susan get better so quickly?

By this the stars were almost gone,
The moon was setting on the hill,
So pale you scarcely looked at her:
415   The little birds began to stir,
Though yet their tongues were still.

The pony, Betty, and her boy,
Wind slowly through the woody dale:
And who is she, be-times abroad.
420   That hobbles up the steep rough road?
Who is it, but old Susan Gale?

Long Susan lay deep lost in thought,
And many dreadful fears beset her,
Both for her messenger and nurse;
425   And as her mind grew worse and worse,
Her body it grew better.

She turned, she toss'd herself in bed,
On all sides doubts and terrors met her;
Point after point did she discuss;
430   And while her mind was fighting thus,
Her body still grew better.

"Alas! what is become of them?
"These fears can never be endured,
"I'll to the wood." – The word scarce said,
435   Did Susan rise up from her bed,
As if by magic cured.

Away she posts up hill and down,
And to the wood at length is come,
She spies her friends, she shouts a greeting;
440   Oh me! it is a merry meeting,
As ever was in Christendom.

Lines
written near Richmond, upon the Thames, at evening

This early poem was probably written before 1791 and redrafted in the Alfoxden year. Here Wordsworth has written a piece in the poetic mode of the eighteenth century. It is useful to see what a conventional poem of the time was like. *Lines* could serve a useful purpose for students as a contrast to the more experimental poems in the volume.

The poem was actually written about the river Cam near Cambridge. It suited Wordsworth's purpose to change the scene so that he could make reference to Collin's *Ode on the Death of Thomson*. The poet Thomson died at Richmond in 1748 and Collins's *Ode* refers to 'Remembrance' haunting the shores of the Thames. In many ways, *Lines* is a very 'literary' poem.

It is a meditation on the transitory nature of life, using the image of a boat on a river. The boat faces the 'rich' glimmering waters to the west, while behind the water is darkened. Wordsworth describes the poet seeing the view and imagining it enduring, instead of as it really is – ephemeral.

1   *imprest* – imprinted.

The owls have hardly sung their last,
While our four travellers homeward wend;
The owls have hooted all night long,
445 And with the owls began my song,
And with the owls must end.

For while they all were travelling home,
Cried Betty, "Tell us Johnny, do,
"Where all this long night you have been,
450 "What you have heard, what you have seen,
"And Johnny, mind you tell us true."

Now Johnny all night long had heard
The owls in tuneful concert strive;
No doubt too he the moon had seen;
455 For in the moonlight he had been
From eight o'clock till five.

And thus to Betty's question, he
Made answer, like a traveller bold,
(His very words I give to you,)
460 "The cocks did crow to-whoo, to-whoo,
"And the sun did shine so cold."
– Thus answered Johnny in his glory,
And that was all his travel's story.

Lines
written near Richmond, upon the Thames, at Evening

How rich the wave, in front, imprest
With evening-twilight's summer hues,
While, facing thus the crimson west,

9   *bard* – poet.
II *deems* – believes, judges.

Look at the personification of the 'stream' in the first two stanzas by examining the words 'smiling', 'beguiling', 'allure'. Wordsworth is ascribing certain human qualities to the river. What are they?

Look at the stanza beginning 'Glide gently'. Can you find any thematic material here that connects up with the rest of Lyrical Ballads?

30 *ditty* – short, simple song.

The boat her silent path pursues!
5   And see how dark the backward stream!
A little moment past, so smiling!
And still, perhaps, with faithless gleam,
Some other loiterer beguiling.

Such views the youthful bard allure,
10   But, heedless of the following gloom,
He deems their colours shall endure
'Till peace go with him to the tomb.
– And let him nurse his fond deceit,

And what if he must die in sorrow!
15   Who would not cherish dreams so sweet,
Though grief and pain may come to-morrow?

Glide gently, thus for ever glide,
O Thames ! that other bards may see,
As lovely visions by thy side
20   As now, fair river! come to me.
Oh glide, fair stream! for ever so;
Thy quiet soul on all bestowing,
'Till all our minds for ever flow,
As thy deep waters now are flowing.

25   Vain thought! yet be as now thou art,
That in thy waters may be seen
The image of a poet's heart,
How bright, how solemn, how serene!
Such heart did once the poet bless,
30   Who, pouring here a * later ditty,
Could find no refuge from distress,
But in the milder grief of pity.

---

* Collin's Ode on the death of Thomson, the last written, I believe of the poems
which were published during his life-time. This Ode is also alluded to in the next
stanza.

Expostulation and Reply

Wordsworth wrote this and its companion piece *The Tables Turned* at the same time in the spring of 1798 at Alfoxden. 'Expostulation' means a friendly remonstration, a gentle ticking-off. The poem is a dialogue with two speakers, 'Matthew' having the first three stanzas to expostulate in and 'William', after the pivotal fourth stanza, replying in the last four. 'Matthew' has generally been taken as a composite figure, based partly on his friend Hazlitt who visited him at Alfoxden in May 1798 while he (Hazlitt) was writing *Essay on the Principles of Human Action*. Wordsworth's old schoolteacher at Hawkshead, William Taylor, is probably also incorporated in 'Matthew', which is perhaps why Wordsworth locates the dialogue at Esthwaite Lake, by Hawkshead, where he spent most of his boyhood. See also the Advertisement for Wordsworth's comments on the origin of these two poems.

What is 'Matthew' accusing 'William' of? Is it laziness? Is it anti-intellectualism? Is it selfishness?

Remembrance! as we glide along,
For him suspend the dashing oar,
35   And pray that never child of Song
May know his freezing sorrows more.
How calm! how still! the only sound,
The dripping of the oar suspended!
– The evening darkness gathers round
40   By virtue's holiest powers attended.

Expostulation and Reply

"Why William, on that old grey stone,
"Thus for the length of half a day,
"Why William, sit you thus alone,
"And dream your time away?

5   "Where are your books? that light bequeath'd
"To beings else forlorn and blind!
"Up! Up! and drink the spirit breath'd
"From dead men to their kind.

"You look round on your mother earth,
10   "As if she for no purpose bore you;
"As if you were her first-born birth,
"And none had lived before you!"

One morning thus, by Esthwaite lake,
When life was sweet I knew not why,
15   To me my good friend Matthew spake,
And thus I made reply.

The Tables Turned

In this sequel to *Expostulation and Reply*, 'William' does the expostulating, but 'Matthew' does not reply.

Compare this poem with Expostulation and Reply. Which poem is more accessible and understandable? Which is more specific?

"The eye it cannot chuse but see,
"We cannot bid the ear be still;
"Our bodies feel, where'er they be,
20 "Against, or with our will.

"Nor less I deem that there are powers,
"Which of themselves our minds impress,
"That we can feed this mind of ours,
"In a wise passiveness.

25 "Think you, mid all this mighty sum
"Of things for ever speaking,
"That nothing of itself will come,
"But we must still be seeking?

"– Then ask not wherefore, here, alone,
30 "Conversing as I may,
"I sit upon this old grey stone,
"And dream my time away."

The Tables Turned;
AN EVENING SCENE, ON THE SAME SUBJECT

Up! up! my friend, and clear your looks,
Why all this toil and trouble?
Up! up! my friend, and quit your books,
Or surely you'll grow double.

5 The sun above the mountain's head,
A freshening lustre mellow,
Through all the long green fields has spread,
His first sweet evening yellow.

10   *woodland linnet* – linnets are not woodland birds. Wordsworth is suggesting all small songbirds here. He was not an authority on birds.

13   *throstle* – song thrush.

21   *vernal* – appearing in spring.

24   *sages* – philosophers.

30   *barren leaves* – sterile, unproductive books.

Books! 'tis a dull and endless strife,
10   Come, hear the woodland linnet,
How sweet his music; on my life
There's more of wisdom in it.

And hark! how blithe the throstle sings!
And he is no mean preacher;
15   Come forth into the light of things,
Let Nature be your teacher.

She has a world of ready wealth,
Our minds and hearts to bless –
Spontaneous wisdom breathed by health,
20   Truth breathed by chearfulness.

One impulse from a vernal wood
May teach you more of man;
Of moral evil and of good,
Than all the sages can.

25   Sweet is the lore which nature brings;
Our meddling intellect
Misshapes the beauteous forms of things;
– We murder to dissect.

Enough of science and of art;
30   Close up these barren leaves;
Come forth, and bring with you a heart
That watches and receives.

Old Man Travelling;
Animal Tranquillity and Decay,
A Sketch

Wordsworth wrote this in 1796–7. He remembered it as 'an overflowing' from *The Old Cumberland Beggar*, a poem he was writing on poverty and vagrancy. In *Old Man Travelling*, Wordsworth concentrates on specific observation of a single figure, met on the road and hailed by the poet.

Consider the sub-title. Do you feel it is an adequate indication of what is happening in the poem?

Is the old man led to 'peace so perfect' (line 13)? Who says so?

Examine the contrast between the first fourteen lines of the poem and the last four. What is the effect of this contrast?

Does Wordsworth invalidate what he himself says about the old man by presenting the old man's answer?

Old Man Travelling;

ANIMAL TRANQUILLITY AND DECAY,

A SKETCH

> The little hedge-row birds,
> That peck along the road, regard him not.
> He travels on, and in his face, his step,
> His gait, is one expression; every limb,
> 5 His look and bending figure, all bespeak
> A man who does not move with pain, but moves
> With thought – He is insensibly subdued
> To settled quiet: he is one by whom
> All effort seems forgotten, one to whom
> 10 Long patience has such mild composure given,
> That patience now doth seem a thing, of which
> He hath no need. He is by nature led
> To peace so perfect, that the young behold
> With envy, what the old man hardly feels.
> 15 – I asked him whither he was bound, and what
> The object of his journey; he replied
> "Sir! I am going many miles to take
> "A last leave of my son, a mariner,
> "Who from a sea-fight has been brought to Falmouth,
> 20 And there is dying in an hospital."

The Complaint
of a forsaken Indian Woman

Wordsworth wrote this at Alfoxden in 1798, after reading Samuel Hearne's *A Journey from Prince of Wales's Fort in Hudson Bay, to the Northern Ocean. Undertaken by Order of the Hudson's Bay Company for the Discovery of Copper Mines, A North West Passage etc in the Years 1769, 1770, 1771 and 1772,* published in 1795. Wordsworth later suggested what he found interesting in the situation – 'the last struggle of a human being, at the approach of death, cleaving in solitude to life and society' (Preface, 1802) – and stated his attempt 'to follow the fluxes and refluxes of the mind when agitated by the great and simple affections of our nature'.

3   *northern gleams* – Northern Lights or Aurora Borealis.

The Complaint
of a forsaken Indian Woman

*[When a Northern Indian, from sickness, is unable to continue his journey
with his companions; he is left behind, covered over with Deer-skins,
and is supplied with water, food, and fuel if the situation of the place
will afford it. He is informed of the track which his companions intend
to pursue, and if he is unable to follow, or overtake them, he perishes
alone in the Desart; unless he should have the good fortune to fall in
with some other Tribes of Indians. It is unnecessary to add that the
females are equally, or still more, exposed to the same fate. See that very
interesting work,* Hearne's Journey *from* Hudson's Bay *to the*
Northern Ocean. *When the Northern Lights, as the same writer
informs us, vary their position in the air, they make a rustling and a
crackling noise. This circumstance is alluded to in the first stanza of the
following poem.]*

> Before I see another day,
> Oh let my body die away!
> In sleep I heard the northern gleams;
> The stars they were among my dreams;
5 > In sleep did I behold the skies,
> I saw the crackling flashes drive;
> And yet they are upon my eyes,
> And yet I am alive.
> Before I see another day,
10 > Oh let my body die away!

25   *my limbs grew stronger* – Hearne's *Journey* describes a woman left behind who 'came up with us three several times, after being left in the manner described. At length, poor creature! she dropt behind, and no one attempted to go back in search of her'.

What is the woman referring to in lines 35–36?

My fire is dead: it knew no pain;
Yet is it dead, and I remain.
All stiff with ice the ashes lie;
And they are dead, and I will die.
15 When I was well, I wished to live,
For clothes, for warmth, for food, and fire;
But they to me no joy can give,
No pleasure now, and no desire.
Then here contented will I lie;
20 Alone I cannot fear to die.

Alas! you might have dragged me on
Another day, a single one!
Too soon despair o'er me prevailed;
Too soon my heartless spirit failed;
25 When you were gone my limbs were stronger,
And Oh how grievously I rue,
That, afterwards, a little longer,
My friends, I did not follow you!
For strong and without pain I lay,
30 My friends, when you were gone away.

My child! they gave thee to another,
A woman who was not thy mother.
When from my arms my babe they took,
On me how strangely did he look!
35 Through his whole body something ran,
A most strange something did I see;
– As if he strove to be a man,
That he might pull the sledge for me.
And then he stretched his arms, how wild
40 Oh mercy! like a little child.

What connections can you find between this poem and other poems in the volume?

Explore the contrasts you find in the poem.

My little joy! my little pride!
In two days more I must have died.
Then do not weep and grieve for me;
I feel I must have died with thee.
45 Oh wind that o'er my head art flying,
The way my friends their course did bend,
I should not feel the pain of dying,
Could I with thee a message send.
Too soon, my friends, you went away;
50 For I had many things to say.

I'll follow you across the snow,
You travel heavily and slow:
In spite of all my weary pain,
I'll look upon your tents again.
55 My fire is dead, and snowy white
The water which beside it stood;
The wolf has come to me to-night,
And he has stolen away my food.
For ever left alone am I,
60 Then wherefore should I fear to die?

My journey will be shortly run,
I shall not see another sun,
I cannot lift my limbs to know
If they have any life or no.
65 My poor forsaken child! if I
For once could have thee close to me,
With happy heart I then would die,
And my last thoughts would happy be.
I feel my body die away,
70 I shall not see another day.

The Convict

This early poem of Wordsworth was probably written between 1793 and 1796. It forms part of the debate on prisons, prisoners and punishment (as do Coleridge's *The Dungeon* and *The Foster-Mother's Tale*) which was widespread in the 1790s. Here Wordsworth clearly agrees with Godwin, who proposed that transportation to the colonies should replace the death penalty.

> *Wordsworth constructs himself as a benevolent visitor to a prison. How does he portray the prisoner? What sort of feelings does the prisoner have?*

The Convict

    The glory of evening was spread through the west;
      – On the slope of a mountain I stood,
    While the joy that precedes the calm season of rest
      Rang loud through the meadow and wood.

5   "And must we then part from a dwelling so fair?"
      In the pain of my spirit I said,
    And with a deep sadness I turned, to repair
      To the cell where the convict is laid.

    The thick-ribbed walls that o'ershadow the gate
10   Resound; and the dungeons unfold:
    I pause; and at length, through the glimmering grate,
      That outcast of pity behold.

    His black matted head on his shoulder is bent,
      And deep is the sigh of his breath,
15 And with stedfast dejection his eyes are intent
      On the fetters that link him to death.

    'Tis sorrow enough on that visage to gaze,
      That body dismiss'd from his care;
    Yet my fancy has pierced to his heart, and pourtrays
20   More terrible images there.

    His bones are consumed, and his life-blood is dried,
      With wishes the past to undo;
    And his crime, through the pains that o'erwhelm him,
      descried,
      Still blackens and grows on his view.

25   *synod* – assembly or meeting for debate.

> What is Wordsworth suggesting in lines 25–9? Why does he mention the 'monarch'?

> Explain the use of the verb 'blossom' in the last line.

32   *disease* – unrest, uneasiness.

25 When from the dark synod, or blood-reeking field,
    To his chamber the monarch is led,
All soothers of sense their soft virtue shall yield,
    And quietness pillow his head.

But if grief, self-consumed, in oblivion would doze,
30   And conscience her tortures appease,
'Mid tumult and uproar this man must repose;
    In the comfortless vault of disease.

When his fetters at night have so press'd on his limbs,
    That the weight can no longer be borne,
35 If, while a half-slumber his memory bedims,
    The wretch on his pallet should turn,

While the jail-mastiff howls at the dull clanking chain,
    From the roots of his hair there shall start
A thousand sharp punctures of cold-sweating pain,
40   And terror shall leap at his heart.

But now he half-raises his deep-sunken eye,
    And the motion unsettles a tear;
The silence of sorrow it seems to supply,
    And asks of me why I am here.

45 "Poor victim! no idle intruder has stood
    "With o'erweening complacence our state to compare,
"But one, whose first wish is the wish to be good,
    "Is come as a brother thy sorrows to share.

"At thy name though compassion her nature resign,
50   "Though in virtue's proud mouth thy report be a stain,
"My care, if the arm of the mighty were mine,
    "Would plant thee where yet thou might'st blossom again."

Lines
written a few miles above Tintern Abbey,
on revisiting the banks of the Wye
during a tour
July 13, 1798

Wordsworth later told Isabella Fenwick about the composition of the poem.

> 'July 1798. No poem of mine was composed under
> circumstances more pleasant for me to remember than this.
> I began it upon leaving Tintern, after crossing the Wye, and
> concluded it just as I was entering Bristol in the evening, after a
> ramble of 4 or 5 days, with my sister. Not a line of it was altered,
> and not any part of it written down til I reached Bristol. It was
> published almost immediately after in the little volume......'
> [*Lyrical Ballads* was first published in Bristol.]

Wordsworth was perhaps simplifying the writing process of the poem as he
recalled it many years later, but certainly the poem was written quickly and
finished as the Wordsworths were entering Bristol. (Wordsworth frequently
composed when he was out of doors and walking.) The poem was handed
over to the publishers and was printed as the last poem in *Lyrical Ballads*.

1   *five years* – Wordsworth first visited the Wye Valley in August 1793.

What mood is developed by the description in the opening lines (lines 1–22)?

Lines
written a few miles above Tintern Abbey,

ON REVISITING THE BANKS OF THE WYE
DURING A TOUR,
July 13, 1798

> Five years have passed; five summers, with the length
> Of five long winters! and again I hear
> These waters, rolling from their mountain-springs
> With a sweet inland murmur. * – Once again
> 5 Do I behold these steep and lofty cliffs,
> Which on a wild secluded scene impress
> Thoughts of more deep seclusion; and connect
> The landscape with the quiet of the sky.
> The day is come when I again repose
> 10 Here, under this dark sycamore, and view
> These plots of cottage-ground, these orchard-tufts,
> Which, at this season, with their unripe fruits,
> Among the woods and copses lose themselves,
> Nor, with their green and simple hue, disturb
> 15 The wild green landscape. Once again I see
> These hedge-rows, hardly hedge-rows, little lines
> Of sportive wood run wild; these pastoral farms
> Green to the very door; and wreathes of smoke
> Sent up, in silence, from among the trees,
> 20 With some uncertain notice, as might seem,

---

*   The river is not affected by the tides a few miles above Tintern.

38 *sublime* – of the most exalted kind, so distinguished by some impressive quality as to inspire awe or wonder. (This is a key word in Romanticism.)

42–50 – This state of near-trance is described by Wordsworth on several occasions. It seems to have been an experience in which the distinction between the human consciousness and the external world is lost. *The Prelude* contains several such moments.

Discuss the effects the memory of the landscape of Tintern Abbey has on the poet (lines 23–48).

Of vagrant dwellers in the houseless woods,
Or of some hermit's cave, where by his fire
The hermit sits alone.

                        Though absent long,
These forms of beauty have not been to me,
25 As is a landscape to a blind man's eye:
But oft, in lonely rooms, and mid the din
Of towns and cities, I have owed to them,
In hours of weariness, sensations sweet,
Felt in the blood, and felt along the heart,
30 And passing even into my purer mind
With tranquil restoration: – feelings too
Of unremembered pleasure; such, perhaps,
As may have had no trivial influence
On that best portion of a good man's life;
35 His little, nameless, unremembered acts
Of kindness and of love. Nor less, I trust,
To them I may have owed another gift,
Of aspect more sublime; that blessed mood,
In which the burthen of the mystery,
40 In which the heavy and the weary weight
Of all this unintelligible world
Is lighten'd: – that serene and blessed mood,
In which the affections gently lead us on,
Until, the breath of this corporeal frame,
45 And even the motion of our human blood
Almost suspended, we are laid asleep
In body, and become a living soul:
While with an eye made quiet by the power
Of harmony, and the deep power of joy,
We see into the life of things.

57   *sylvan* – wooded, flowing through trees.

68   *roe* – deer.

50   If this
Be but a vain belief, yet, oh! how oft,
In darkness, and amid the many shapes
Of joyless day-light; when the fretful stir
Unprofitable, and the fever of the world,
55 Have hung upon the beatings of my heart,
How oft, in spirit, have I turned to thee
O sylvan Wye! Thou wanderer through the woods,
How often has my spirit turned to thee!

And now, with gleams of half-extinguish'd thought,
60 With many recognitions dim and faint,
And somewhat of a sad perplexity,
The picture of the mind revives again:
While here I stand, not only with the sense
Of present pleasure, but with pleasing thoughts
65 That in this moment there is life and food
For future years. And so I dare to hope
Though changed, no doubt, from what I was, when first
I came among these hills; when like a roe
I bounded o'er the mountains, by the sides
70 Of the deep rivers, and the lonely streams,
Wherever nature led; more like a man
Flying from something that he dreads, than one
Who sought the thing he loved. For nature then
(The coarser pleasures of my boyish days,
75 And their glad animal movements all gone by,)
To me was all in all. – I cannot paint
What then I was. The sounding cataract
Haunted me like a passion: the tall rock,
The mountain, and the deep and gloomy wood,
80 Their colours and their forms, were then to me
An appetite: a feeling and a love,
That had no need of a remoter charm,
By thought supplied, or any interest

84 *That time is past* – Wordsworth mourns the loss of the visionary experiences of his younger self in several poems, notably *Ode: Intimations of Immortality*.

107 This is a reference to Young's *Night Thoughts* which contains the line 'And half-create the wondrous world they see' ('they' are the senses).

Unborrowed from the eye. – That time is past,
85 And all its aching joys are now no more,
And all its dizzy raptures. Not for this
Faint I, nor mourn nor murmur: other gifts
Have followed, for such loss, I would believe,
Abundant recompence. For I have learned
90 To look on nature, not as in the hour
Of thoughtless youth, but hearing oftentimes
The still, sad music of humanity,
Not harsh nor grating, though of ample power
To chasten and subdue. And I have felt
95 A presence that disturbs me with the joy
Of elevated thoughts; a sense sublime
Of something far more deeply interfused,
Whose dwelling is the light of setting suns,
And the round ocean, and the living air,
100 And the blue sky, and in the mind of man,
A motion and a spirit, that impels
All thinking things, all objects of all thought,
And rolls through all things. Therefore am I still
A lover of the meadows and the woods,
105 And mountains; and of all that we behold
From this green earth; of all the mighty world
Of eye and ear, both what they half-create,*
And what perceive; well pleased to recognize
In nature and the language of the sense,
110 The anchor of my purest thoughts, the nurse,
The guide, the guardian of my heart, and soul
Of all my moral being.

                              Nor, perchance,
If I were not thus taught, should I the more
Suffer my genial spirits to decay:
For thou art with me, here, upon the banks

* This line has a close resemblance to an admirable line of Young, the exact
expression of which I cannot recollect.

116 *my dearest Friend* – his sister Dorothy. Wordsworth suggests that she is still
having the visionary experiences that he has lost.

147 *exhortations* – earnest address or urging.

Of this fair river; thou, my dearest Friend,
My dear, dear Friend, and in thy voice I catch
The language of my former heart, and read
My former pleasures in the shooting lights
120 Of thy wild eyes. Oh! yet a little while
May I behold in thee what I was once,
My dear, dear Sister! And this prayer I make,
Knowing that Nature·never did betray
The heart that loved her; 'tis her privilege,
125 Through all the years of this our life, to lead
From joy to joy: for she can so inform
The mind that is within us, so impress
With quietness and beauty, and so feed
With lofty thoughts, that neither evil tongues,
130 Rash judgments, nor the sneers of selfish men,
Nor greetings where no kindness is, nor all
The dreary intercourse of daily life,
Shall e'er prevail against us, or disturb
Our chearful faith that all which we behold
135 Is full of blessings. Therefore let the moon
Shine on thee in thy solitary walk;
And let the misty mountain winds be free
To blow against thee: and in after years,
When these wild ecstasies shall be matured
140 Into a sober pleasure, when thy mind
Shall be a mansion for all lovely forms,
Thy memory be as a dwelling-place
For all sweet sounds and harmonies; Oh! then,
If solitude, or fear, or pain, or grief,
145 Should be thy portion, with what healing thoughts
Of tender joy wilt thou remember me,
And these my exhortations! Nor, perchance,
If I should be, where I no more can hear
Thy voice, nor catch from thy wild eyes these gleams
150 Of past existence, wilt thou then forget
That on the banks of this delightful stream

Discuss the structure of the poem in relation to one of its main preoccupations – Time:

What was the poet's response to the landscape on his first visit? (lines 67–86)

What is the nature of his 'loss' (line 88)?

Describe what he calls his 'recompense' (line 89).

What does his sister represent (lines 116–60)?

We stood together; and that I, so long
A worshipper of Nature, hither came,
Unwearied in that service: rather say
155 With warmer love, oh! with far deeper zeal
Of holier love. Nor wilt thou then forget,
That after many wanderings, many years
Of absence, these steep woods and lofty cliffs,
And this green pastoral landscape, were to me
160 More dear, both for themselves, and for thy sake.

BACKGROUND

1797–8: The Year of the *Lyrical Ballads*

Lyrical Ballads is the result of one of the most famous collaborations in literature. There were three contributors – all in their mid-twenties in 1797 – Samuel Taylor Coleridge, William Wordsworth and Dorothy Wordsworth. Dorothy's help in the collaboration should not be under-estimated. *Lyrical Ballads* developed from the sustained conversations the three shared during the twelve months from the day in June 1797 when Coleridge arrived breathlessly at Racedown, leaping over a gate and bounding down through a field.

All three were delighted with each other. The two men were temperamental opposites: Coleridge, enthusiastic, talkative and brilliant, William meditative and self-sufficient. Dorothy was watchful, direct and ardent. Dorothy said of Coleridge 'He is a wonderful man. His conversation teems with soul, mind and spirit'. Coleridge said of William 'Wordsworth is a great man', and of Dorothy 'her eye watchful in minutest observation of nature.' Her responsiveness to the natural world was valued by both poets. The Journal she began six months later was both a record and source material for them.

The Wordsworths at this time were living at a friend's house in Racedown, Dorset. Dorothy had been separated from her brother when they were orphaned in childhood. She had spent tedious years with relatives, making herself useful about the house. But in 1794 she had been able to join William and act as housekeeper, secretary and companion. He had needed this sort of stability. He was in a state of near breakdown after a series of experiences very different from anything she had seen in her quiet years of genteel drudgery. He had been a firm supporter of the French Revolution and had spent time in Revolutionary France in the early 1790s. He had also been involved with a French girl, Annette Vallon, who had given birth to his daughter. But he was now beginning a long process of re-examination and questioning of his left-wing opinions and rationalist philosophy. He had seen how 'Reason' had led to the excesses of the Terror in France, and how the country in which it had seemed 'bliss to be alive' in the early days of the Revolution was now transformed into a military dictatorship, with Napoleon laying waste the rest of Europe and preparing to invade Britain.

Coleridge was also a radical. He had been politically active in journalism and public lectures. His earlier vision had been the setting up of a commune in America – a self-supporting community without private property, where a group of friends could live in peace, bringing up their children and working on the land without servants. He called it Pantisocracy, meaning a society ruled equally by all. Coleridge had spent some time on plans for this, but by 1797 the idea had been abandoned. He had married in preparation for the scheme, and now lived with his wife Sara and their baby son in a tiny cottage in Nether Stowey in the Quantock Hills in Somerset. He too was re-examining his life, his beliefs and his ambitions.

All were concerned with what Coleridge called the 'two giants yclept Bread and Cheese'. Neither of the men was rich. At a time when a 'skilled worker such as a printer earned approximately £90 a year, while a gentleman with a small household and a servant in London could live comfortably on £200 a year' (Holmes *160*), Coleridge and Wordsworth were saved from poverty only by the kindness of friends. A friend of Coleridge had left him an annuity of £40 a year. The debt-ridden Wordsworth had been helped by a legacy of £900, but he and Dorothy were living very frugally and were not relieved from anxiety until William's inheritance was settled in 1802. It had been blocked by a powerful Lake District landowner, Lord Lonsdale.

By the time Coleridge had returned home, walking the forty miles to Nether Stowey, he was determined to bring the Wordsworths nearer. Perhaps he still had the idea of establishing a community of like-minded people – a poetic commune. By mid-July he had accomplished this. The Wordsworths moved to a house four ' miles way, renting Alfoxden House for £23 per annum. They stayed for a year. This was the year of *Lyrical Ballads*.

Coleridge issued invitations to so many other friends that local people became convinced that some sort of radical community was being established. The Home Office sent a special agent down to investigate. He followed them, taking notes of their activities. They were obviously suspicious characters – walking at night; gazing out to sea; writing furiously and then reading out loud what they had written; taking long walking expeditions; closely examining rocks and streams and flowers;

and reading some very subversive literature. Local people were uncon-
vinced even that Dorothy was William's sister. The agent's report of
August 1797 described them as 'a mischievous gang of disaffected Eng-
lishmen' and a 'sett of violent Democrats'.

It would be a mistake to imagine that these three wandered in idyllic
surroundings, untouched by political realities. The England of 1797–8
was at war with an unstoppable European neighbour (France), with no
allies left on the Continent, and on the verge of defeat. Added to this
were a disastrous campaign in the West Indies, bad harvests, loss of
markets, soaring prices, naval mutinies and a French fleet prevented
only by bad weather from invading an Ireland seething with rebellion.
All this is the context of *Lyrical Ballads*.

One of Dorothy's letters dated 20th November, 1797 mentions an idea
about publication.

We have been on another (walking) tour: we set out last Monday evening
(13 Nov) at half past four. The evening was dark and cloudy; we went about
eight miles, William and Coleridge employing themselves in laying the plan
of a ballad, to be published with some poems of William's.

Wordsworth later remembered 'as our united funds were very small,
we agreed to defray the expense of the tour by writing a Poem ......in the
course of this walk was planned the Poem of The Ancient Mariner'.
When *Lyrical Ballads* was published anonymously in October 1798,
this was the first poem of the collection.

Social and Political Background

Introduction

The sixty years of George III's reign (1760–1820), which saw the rise and development of English Romanticism, is one of the most revolutionary in British history. The population virtually doubled. Massive changes in land use and ownership ('The Agrarian revolution') provided the means to feed an increasing population, but at a great social cost. The poor lost their right to grazing on the common land, and many poorer farmers were squeezed out as Acts of Enclosure increased year by year.

Old structures of power and deference were challenged more and more. The American Revolution (1776) seemed to demonstrate the validity of Enlightenment political thought. The French Revolution (1798) seemed to confirm this, being initially hailed with delight by the younger generation and many of their elders. Human nature seemed perfectible and general happiness obtainable. The collapse of the French Revolution into massacres and atrocities (Reign of Terror 1792–4) and French wars of aggression on neighbouring countries betrayed the hopes of a generation. This is the background to the crisis of many young intellectuals as well as Coleridge and Wordsworth. Romanticism developed in a harsh period of social discontent and near revolution, sharpened by the deprivation of war with France (1793–1815, with one short break in 1802.)

Chronology

1760 Accession of George III.

Beginnings of the Industrial Revolution:
1769 Joseph Wedgwood opens pottery factory at Etruria near Stoke; James Watt patents steam engine; Richard Arkwright invents water-powered spinning frame.
1770 James Hargreaves invents the spinning jenny.
1776 Adam Smith *The Wealth of Nations*, the classic defence of the free market, unimpeded trade and economic expansion.
From 1740s the population rises rapidly until it doubles (about 10.5 million) by 1800.
1765 'Wilkes and Liberty' riots in London, the first clear sign of a prolonged social crisis.

1770s Increasing demand for Parliamentary Reform.
Signs of dislocation and strain within social system, alterations within its economic structures.

1776 *Declaration of American Independence*:
The crucial challenge to hierarchical and traditional views of power. Assertion of 'self-evident' equality of men, their 'right to happiness', their right to overthrow governments which do not serve the interests of those they govern. These ideas had been gathering strength since John Locke's *Two Treatises on Civil Government*, 1690, but they now became practical politics and confirm a growing belief at the end of the eighteenth century in the perfectibility of man through Reason.

1783 American War ended with British recognition of the independence of the United States.

1783 – 1801 William Pitt Prime Minister – up to 1792 a competent manager of the nation's finances and a moderate reformer. After beginning of French War, a somewhat unsuccessful war leader, pursuing a policy of repressing internal discontent.

1789 *The French Revolution:*
Convening of Three Estates in France; Fall of the Bastille July 14th; Declaration of the Rights of Man; King and Royal Family seized at Versailles and taken to Paris. Most English opinion at first highly favourable – 'How much the greatest thing that has ever happened in the world and how much the best' (Charles James Fox, Whig leader).
The Bastille prison had been a symbol of repression for many years:-

What English Heart would not rejoice
To hear that thou wert fall'n at last.
(Cowper)

1790 July 14th: first anniversary of the Revolution celebrated with scenes of rejoicing. Louis XVI acclaimed as constitutional monarch. Wordsworth sees this public joy on his first visit to France, a walking tour including the Alps and Italy in 1790.

1791 Attempted flight of Louis XVI to Varennes after attacks on the Church. He is recaptured and brought back to Paris. The turning point of the French Revolution. Power passes into the hands of the extremists.

1791–2 Wordsworth spends year in France, fired with enthusiasm for republican ideals:

Bliss was it in that dawn to be alive
But to be young was very Heaven
(*The Prelude* 1850, Book 11, lines 108–9)

In Blois Wordsworth became friendly with Beaupuy, a captain in the Republican army and a sincere idealist, under whose influence he became an ardent Republican and Democrat. Wordsworth also fell in love with Annette Vallon, a French girl who bore him a daughter.

1791 First signs of conservative reaction against French Revolution in England. 'Church and King' mob sack home of radical philosopher Joseph Priestley in Birmingham.

1792 Armies of Austria and Prussia invade France. September Massacres of innocent women and children in Paris. Beginning of the Reign of Terror (September 1792 – July 1794). Mass executions in Paris, Bordeaux, Lyons, the Vendée, of 'enemies of the people'.

1793 France declares war on Britain. Wordsworth separated from Annette and his child. Execution of Louis XVI and Marie Antoinette.

1793–6 Period of deep distress approaching mental breakdown for Wordsworth: guilt over Annette, rejection of his political ideals by his family, but perhaps most of all, gradual realization that his beliefs in Reason and human perfectibility (the beliefs of his generation and the growing hopes of the eighteenth century) were ending in horrors and atrocities in France.

Domestic carnage now filled the whole year....
Head after head, and never heads enough
For those that bade them fall....

O Friend!
It was a lamentable time for man
Whether a hope had e'er been his or not!
A woeful time for them whose hopes survived
The shock, most woeful for those few who still
Were flattered, and had trust in human kind.
(*The Prelude*, Book 10, lines 355 – 88)

(Wordsworth's feelings may be guessed by analogy with the emotional effects of the failure of Communism in the twentieth century.)

1793 Destruction of the Girondins (moderate idealistic Republicans).

1794 Jacobins (extreme Republicans) turn on themselves. Execution of Danton, then fall of Robespierre.

France defeats the armies of invading monarchies and secures the Revolution in Battle of Fleurus. After this, the French military machine dominates Europe for the next twenty years.

In Britain the Habeas Corpus Act is suspended. (Habeas Corpus guarantees an accused person the right of prompt indictment or quick release.)

1795 France conquers the Netherlands and the Rhineland.

1796 France invades Italy. Napoleon establishes his reputation as a military commander.

1797 French pillage and seizure of small harmless states of Venice
1798 and Switzerland.

See Wordsworth's *On the Extinction of the Venetian Republic* and Coleridge's *France, an Ode*. France's military ruthlessness and dominance led to the complete disillusionment of Wordsworth and Coleridge with the French Revolution.

But now, become oppressors in their turn,
Frenchmen had changed a war of self-defence
For one of conquest, losing sight of all
Which they had struggled for.
(*The Prelude*, Book 11, lines 206 – 9)

1795 Two Acts passed in Britain, forbidding seditious meetings and treasonable conspiracy. Panic at French Revolution and failure of military effort against it leads to increasingly repressive measures and suppression of radical thought and activity by the British ruling class.

1796 Spain and Holland make peace with France and become her allies. France is now invincible on land and threatening invasion of Britain. British fleet withdraws from Mediterranean.

1797 Year of crisis. British naval mutinies at the Nore and Spithead briefly leave country defenceless against France. Ireland in state of revolt awaits French help which only a storm in Bantry Bay prevents. Treaty of Campo Formio between France and Austria establishes French satellite republics in Northern Italy.

1798 Rebellion in Ireland crushed. France invades Egypt. French fleet destroyed by Nelson at Battle of the Nile. Worst crisis of the war (1797–8) over.

1799 Military coup in France. Napoleon Bonaparte becomes First Consul, effectively dictator.

1800 French victories at Hohenlinden and Marengo.

1802–3 Peace of Amiens. A brief truce in French War allows Wordsworth to visit France.

1804 Napoleon hereditary Emperor of France.

1805 British naval victory at Trafalgar ends all fear of French invasion.

1807 Abolition of the Slave Trade in British Dominions. France invades Spain and Portugal.

1808 Revolt in Spain the first serious blow against Napoleon's Empire. British land troops in Portugal. Convention of Cintra allows French withdrawal. Wordsworth, now a strong patriot, produces energetic political pamphlet attacking the Convention.

1809 Successful campaign against French army begins with Wellington Commander in Chief of British forces in Spain.

1810 Deepening trade recession in Britain due to Napoleon barring the Continent to British goods.

1811 George III hopelessly insane. Prince of Wales installed as Regent.

1812 Luddites attack textile frames and factories. Napoleon invades Russia and is forced to retreat with appalling losses.

1813 Wellington liberates Spain. French driven from Holland, Italy, Switzerland.

1814 Allied armies invade France. Fall of Paris. Exile of Napoleon to Elba. Congress of Vienna reconstitutes Europe on conservative principles. Stephenson invents first locomotive.

1815 Napoleon escapes from Elba, returns to France, is defeated at Waterloo.

1816 Severe economic depression.

1817 Suspension of Habeas Corpus. Stern government repression.

1819 Peterloo Massacre. Six Acts against radical activity.

1820 Death of George III.

Cultural and Literary Background

Introduction

From the middle of the eighteenth century, new themes entered literature. Interest in the socially excluded and dispossessed; in wild, rugged 'sublime' scenery; in the meditations of the solitary rather than the man in the community; in earlier historical times such as the Middle Ages; and in horror and the supernatural, began to alter fundamentally the subject matter of what people read and talked about. The political revolution of the 1790s quickened this. At the same time, political discourse became polarised into the 'Left' and 'Right' in a way we can understand today.

Chronology

Sensibility

1740s A new sensitivity to the lives and sufferings of excluded groups – the rural poor, children, animals, the mentally afflicted and women. Key texts: Richardson, *Pamela* (1739), *Joseph Andrews* (1742), and *Clarissa* (1748) – texts about a servant girl, a footman and a middle-class woman respectively.

The Sublime

Edmund Burke, *A Philosophical Enquiry into the Origin of our Ideas of the Sublime and Beautiful* (1757) – one of several works which discuss the aesthetic value of grandeur, terror, and rugged, wild scenery as more potent than the regular and harmonious.

Poetry: new directions

James Thomson *The Seasons* (1726–30).

Edward Young *The Complaint or Night Thoughts on Life, Death and Immortality* (1742–5).

Bishop Percy, *Reliques of Early English Poetry* (1764) signals rise of interest in the historical, especially mediaeval, past and in older 'naive' forms such as the ballad.

Thomas Gray *Elegy written in a Country Churchyard* (1751) where the poet reflects in solitude on the common human condition.

William Collins *Ode on Popular Superstitions of the Highlands* (published 1788) shows interest in 'primitive', legendary beliefs of remote country districts. Also concept of poetry as visionary and sacred.

William Cowper *The Task* (1785) – a poetry of reverie, reflection and natural description.

William Lisle Bowles **Fourteen Sonnets** (1789) – meditations on picturesque locations and scenery.

1790 Edmund Burke **Reflections on the Revolution in France** – powerfully argued attack on the actual premises of the Revolution, i.e. the perfectibility of man and the power of Reason to break with the past and remake societies and political organizations. Burke instead asserts History against Reason; slow organic development against sudden theory-based change. He is the founder of philosophical conservatism and of the conservative strain in Romanticism.

1791 Thomas Paine **The Rights of Man Part 1** – vigorous answer to Burke. Assertion of the power of Reason and common sense to demolish cruel and wasteful frauds of authority. Kingship and aristocracy mere frauds – men naturally equal. Burke and Paine define fundamental ideological division of Romantic period.

1792 Mary Wollstonecraft **A Vindication of the Rights of Women** – the first significant text to question masculine and feminine roles and identities, male power and discourse. Example of the radicalization of politics in the 1790s.

1793 William Godwin **An Enquiry concerning Political Justice** – a radical text affirming that all rational human beings must be benevolent. 'Truth is omnipotent...Man is perfectible.'

Hannah Moore **Village Politics** – one of several influential pamphlets in simple language for mass readership; attacks French Revolutionary ideals as irreligious and absurd.

1793 William Wordsworth *Descriptive Sketches* and *An Evening Walk*. These pieces were heard and admired by Coleridge.

1794 William Blake **Songs of Innocence and Experience, The First Book of Urizen, Europe** – attacks on the tyranny of Reason, Enlightenment and repressive interpretations of Christianity.

William Godwin **Caleb Williams** – powerful novel indicting social oppression.

Thomas Paine **The Age of Reason** – rationalist attack on Christianity.

Ann Radcliffe **The Mysteries of Udolpho** – one of the best-known Gothic novels; terrors of solitary imagination and the solace of landscape.

1794 Coleridge *Reflections on having left a Place of Retirement* – poem which attempts simple diction and conversational ease. Coleridge was interested in ideas of philosopher David Hartley (1705–57) whose *Observations on Man* (1749) denied that the moral sense was innate and traced it instead to an 'association of ideas'. According to this theory, the mind is passive and receptive. The environment acts upon the mind and the moral sense develops from these experiences (hence the importance of a natural and beneficent environment). Coleridge called his first son after Hartley and his influence can be seen in *The Nightingale* and *Frost at Midnight*. This theory also became central to Wordsworth's poetry, and must be borne in mind when reading *Lyrical Ballads*.

Coleridge fairly soon began to reject Hartley's theories in favour of those of George Berkeley (1685–1753) and the intuitions of mystics such as Jacob Boehme (1575–1624). These writers confirmed Coleridge's belief in the essential ordering and creative power of the mind. In Berkeley's view, spirit is the only real cause or power. These ideas are reflected in Coleridge's *Dejection: an Ode* (1802) where he states 'And in our life alone does Nature live' (line 48).

1796 Coleridge *Poems on Various Subjects* includes *The Eolian Harp*, an early 'Conversation' poem.

1798 Thomas Malthus *Principles of Population* asserts 'iron law of wages' – that the population (growing geometrically) will always tend to outrun means of subsistence (growing arithmetically). Signals new and ruthless 'science' of Political Economy in developing industrial society.

1797–1798 The year of the *Lyrical Ballads*.

The division of the labour is discussed by Coleridge in Chapter XIV of *Biographia Literaria* (1817). There was to be a series of poems 'of two sorts':

In the one, the incidents and agents were to be, in part at least, supernatural; and the excellence aimed at was to consist in the interesting of the affections by the dramatic truth of such emotions, as would naturally accompany such situations, supposing them to be real.....For the second class, subjects were to be chosen from ordinary life; the characters and incidents were to be such as will be found in every village and its vicinity, where there is a meditative and feeling mind to seek after them, or to notice them, when they present themselves.

Coleridge was to deal with the first, Wordsworth the second.

1800, 1802 Second and third editions of *Lyrical Ballads*. More poems were added. The most significant feature of these editions is the Preface written by Wordsworth from ideas developed by Coleridge. Wordsworth extended the brief Advertisement of 1798 into a long justification of the experiments of the volume. The expanded 1802 Preface is one of the key documents of Romanticism.

1. Wordsworth defends his use of the language and situations of common life by stating that his intention was to trace 'the primary laws of our nature, chiefly as far as regards the manner in which we associate ideas in a state of excitement'. 'Low and rustic life' gives him a better opportunity to do this because 'elementary feelings exist in a state of greater simplicity.....and are more durable' because of the nature of 'rural occupations'. Also because of their surroundings 'the passions of men are incorporated with the beautiful and permanent forms of nature'. For the same reasons, the language of such men 'is more permanent and far more philosophic' than that 'frequently substituted for it by Poets'.

2. Wordsworth makes a sustained attack on contemporary urban society and culture. This has been particularly influential. 'For a multitude of causes unknown to former times are now acting with a combined force to blunt the discriminating powers of the mind, and unfitting it for all voluntary exertion to reduce it to a state of almost savage torpor. The most effective of these causes are the great national events which are daily taking place, and the increasing accumulation of men in cities, where the uniformity of their occupations produces a craving for extraordinary incident.' (This attack on industrialized mass urban culture remained part of English studies until the 1960s.)

3. Wordsworth also defines the characteristics of Poetry and the Poet in statements which influenced how these were regarded for at least a hundred years.

'Poetry is the spontaneous overflow of powerful feelings; it takes its origin from emotion recollected in tranquillity, the emotion is contemplated till by a species of reaction the tranquillity gradually disappears and an emotion, similar to that which was before the subject of contemplation, is gradually produced, and does itself actually exist in the mind.

What is a Poet?......He is a man speaking to men; a man, it is true, endued with more lively sensibility, more enthusiasm and tenderness, who has a greater knowledge of human nature, and a more comprehensive soul than are supposed to be common among mankind.'

This construction of the Poet as a man set apart by his special qualities – a 'universal' representative of the human race and yet with more 'soul' – has remained current, as has the idea of poetry as something 'spontaneous' and emotional (although Wordsworth does not say this). Feminist critics have taken exception to the way this definition of a poet tacitly excludes women.

Coleridge was to produce a substantial critique of Wordsworth's Preface years later in *Biographia Literaria* (1817), but he voiced his misgivings at the time in letters. He objected to two points in particular. He felt that the 'association of ideas' theory of Hartley, which Wordsworth used to explain the psychology of poetry, was inadequate. Coleridge preferred Berkeley's theories on the innate creative powers of the mind. Secondly, Coleridge came to doubt that rural scenes did purify the heart and feelings. This was not borne out by his own experiences of farmers and rustics.

1802 Scott *Minstrelsy of the Scottish Border*.

1807 Wordsworth *Poems in Two Volumes*.

1816 Coleridge *Christabel and Other Poems*.

1817 Coleridge *Biographia Literaria*.

CRITICAL APPROACHES

Explorations and Activities

The Rime of the Ancyent Marinere

There have been many critical interpretations of this poem. The following are most popular (see also Holmes):

1 Mariner as Coleridge. This biographical approach sees Coleridge, his opium addiction and his depressive illness, as the Mariner with his trials and hallucinations. The albatross is sometimes seen as representing his wife, Sara. He is 'saved' by returning to the community of his friends. To follow up this approach, you will need far more information about the poet.

> It might be useful here to look at the psychology of the Mariner. Look at his actions in the narrative. How much does the Mariner initiate? Is it just the one vital act? Can he be seen as a passive figure?

2 Mariner as Romantic Poet. The Mariner is seen as the artist who goes beyond the normal and conventional restraints of society in his quest for knowledge and art. He passes through terrible trials of loneliness and self-doubt, but is saved by his spontaneous act of sympathy and imagination. He is tormented by the artistic compulsion to re-tell his story.

It is worth noting here that *The Ancient Mariner* (as it was afterwards spelled) greatly influenced Mary Shelley's story of **Frankenstein** (1818). Her frame story is about seamen travelling beyond the known world to polar regions and being caught in ice, while Frankenstein moves intellectually beyond conventional morality when he creates his monster. The tragic/heroic figure of the man who goes beyond the boundaries into the unknown and returns with knowledge bought at the cost of terrible experience is a familiar Romantic one.

> You could follow this up by finding all the references in the poem for crossing boundaries and frontiers (in all senses), moving from the known to the unknown. Look also for the overlap of natural and supernatural spheres.

3 Mariner as Sinner in a religious universe. This interpretation sees the murder of the albatross as a sin against God, or in a more 'green' myth, sin against Nature. His sufferings are necessary and purgatorial, but he

is accepted back into the Church or Community of the Good through the Hermit's absolution.

> You can find plenty of evidence for this approach in the Christian references in the poem. Look also at the dualist pairs – sun and moon, killing and blessing, solitude and company etc.

4 Mariner as Victim of an irrational universe. If the game of dice is seen as important, it suggests a capricious universe driven by chance, where punishment is as arbitrary and sadistic as the initial act of shooting the albatross.

> You can follow this up by looking at cause and effect in the narrative. Is it obvious or not? What makes things happen? For example, does the bird guide the boat out of the ice? Certainly the boat gets out of the ice, but is it a coincidence? What do the Crew die of? Why? Do their deaths depend on the roll of a dice? Why? Is it meaningful or absurd?

5 Mariner as Hero of a sea shanty. It is important to remember that the poem is a ballad and tells a primitive tale. It would be useful to look at some old ballads (e.g. *Sir Patrick Spens*) to get an idea of the genre that Coleridge was using.

The older folk ballads were part of an oral tradition dating back at least to the thirteenth century. The stanza form probably came from mediaeval France. This was generally four lines of eight, six, eight, six syllables, rhyming *a b c b* or *a b a b*. The ballad is basically a narrative. It tells a story, and the simple stanza form is well adapted to this. The story is frequently presented from a narrative point of view and with little description. Dialogue and refrain are typical features.

Ballads were 'rediscovered' by the sophisticated in the eighteenth century, collected and published. Bishop Percy's **Reliques of Ancient English Poetry** (1765) is the most famous example. Late eighteenth-century poets were enthusiastic about the stylized simplicity of the form and its folk origins, as well as the inclusion of the supernatural in its content.

> Isolate the elements in *The Rime of the Ancyent Marinere* that make it a ballad. What techniques does Coleridge use to increase and decrease the pace of the poem? (For example, look at Part III lines 139–53 for increase of pace and lines 159–72 for decrease of pace. Look at rhyme, rhythm and punctuation.)

The Foster-Mother's Tale

The central theme of *Lyrical Ballads* is the link between the human being and the natural world – how necessary and life-giving this is. The Mariner broke this link. In this dramatic fragment, Coleridge shows that Nature alone (and solitary learning) is not enough. Nature should also include human nature. The 'poor mad youth' has not established the link with his fellow human beings. A landscape should include a human community.

> *The Foster-Mother's Tale* is a fragment from a play, written in blank verse. Blank verse is unrhymed iambic pentameter. This means that every line has ten syllables with a pattern of five metric units (unstressed syllable, stressed syllable etc.)
>
> ᵕ / ᵕ / ᵕ　　 / ᵕ /ᵕ /
> e.g. 'And all the Autumn twas his only play').

> What does it remind you of? Does the fact that this is in the form of drama, with character and dialogue, influence the way you read and understand it? Follow up the theme of the solitary by comparing this figure with the one in *Lines left upon a seat in a Yew-tree*. Follow up the theme of prison by comparing this prisoner with the victims of *The Dungeon* and *The Convict*.

Lines left upon a Seat in a Yew-tree which stands near the Lake of Esthwaite

Critics suggest that this poem represents Wordsworth's rejection of the self-sufficiency of Godwin's rationalism (see **Cultural and Literary Background**, page 215). He shows its sterile arrogance. He shows also that Nature is not enough. It should include human nature.

The poem also represents a gifted man neglected by the world and resenting it. There may be some self-reference here. To bury oneself in Nature seems an obvious response for a Romantic, but Wordsworth shows the egotism and self-pity inherent in this. The poem seems to criticize the cult of Sensibility and the Sublime (see **Cultural and Literary Background**) as well as Godwin's idea that society alone is responsible for human imperfections and vice.

> Follow this up by comparing this character with the one in *The Foster-Mother's Tale*. Describe the form of the poem.

The Nightingale, A Conversation Poem

After writing this, Coleridge sent a comic verse letter to Wordsworth which included the following lines:

In stale blank verse a subject stale
I send per post my nightingale.

The letter, like the poem, shows Coleridge's awareness that he was working within a familiar convention, where both style and subject were well-worn already. An early critic saw this poem's relation to Cowper's *The Task* (1785), which Coleridge admired and called 'divine chit chat'.

However, the 'Conversation' poem, though developing from an eighteenth-century model, is one of the two distinctive contributions Coleridge made to poetry, both evident in this volume. The first is more famous – the fantastic and supernatural pieces, exemplified here by *The Rime of the Ancyent Marinere*. *Cristabel* and *Kubla Khan* are other examples. The second contribution is the 'Conversation' poem – an intimate meditation in blank verse which moves from a specific occasion and locality into the past, into reflection on more general matters, projects into the future, and then returns upon itself to a specific time and place. It always sounds autobiographical, but care should be taken about making this assumption. Other Coleridge conversation poems are *Frost at Midnight* and *This Lime Tree Bower my Prison*, both written at this time. It is this extended blank verse form that Wordsworth uses in *Tintern Abbey*. These conversation poems have in common the preoccupation that Coleridge in a letter to Sotheby in 1802 called the 'one life':

'Nature has her proper interest; and he will know what it is, who believes and feels, that every Thing has a Life of its own, and that we are all one life. A Poet's heart and Intellect should be combined, intimately combined and unified, with the great appearances in Nature....'

Explore the concept of the 'one life' in *The Nightingale*.

Look at the mood of the opening of the poem. What effect does it have? Why does Coleridge produce this particular effect?

Look at the way 'moonlight', 'breeze' and 'birdsong' are used in the poem.

Look at the therapeutic powers of Nature in the poem.

The Female Vagrant

The most important characteristic of this poem is its radical content. It is a very explicit attack on contemporary society. It attacks acquisitive landowners, urban unemployment and colonial wars. The female as child and the gypsies are shown as living in harmony with a beneficent natural world. Crime is seen as the result of social oppression.

> This portrait of suffering can be connected up with other pictures of the destitute and abandoned in *Lyrical Ballads*, victims of a corrupt and corrupting system. Note how many of them are women. Look in the **Bibliography** for further accounts of the American revolution, agrarian reform, growth of the towns and the position of women.

Coleridge persuaded Wordsworth to include this in *Lyrical Ballads*, after he had seen it in the longer *Salisbury Plain*, from which it is extracted. Coleridge thought that *Salisbury Plain* was a great new poem.

The poem is written in the style of Spenser. That is, each stanza has three rhymes only in a nine-line unit. The ten-syllable iambic line changes at the end of each stanza to twelve syllables. The poem contains some examples of popular eighteenth-century stylistic characteristics, for example, the personifications of line 157–62.

> Compare the poem to *Last of the Flock* or *Old Man Travelling* to bring out stylistic differences.

Goody Blake and Harry Gill

This poem turns on a curse. Gill's punishment fits his crime (social as well as personal) of withholding fuel from the poor. But he is also protecting his own property. The fact that he first chooses to go into the cold to catch the old woman perhaps shows a particular psychological condition of coldness.

> Compare Gill with the Mariner.

Another approach is to compare this poem with the 'moral verse' current at the time. It has been suggested (Gravil) that the poem is 'openly parodic' of the fashion to write morally improving verse for the edification of the lower classes. Contemporary sententious verse is subverted by a poem which punishes the law-abiding farmer, and not the thief.

Another way to look at the poem is to follow up its connections with the ballad form.

Lines written at a small distance from my House, and sent by my little Boy to the Person to whom they are addressed

This celebrates Wordsworth's intense experience of the natural world in spring and his sustained conviction that if the individual responds to Nature, then a relationship is established between Nature and the self which is immensely beneficial to the human. The penultimate stanza celebrates the 'blessed power' in language which sounds religious, but its reference is natural rather than Christian.

> Compare this poem with *Lines written in early Spring*, or *Expostulation and Reply* and *The Tables Turned*.

Simon Lee, the old Huntsman

Critics have disagreed about this poem. Contemporary reviewers felt the subject matter unworthy of artistic treatment. Modern critics have pointed out its ambiguities of tone.

'It is as though the reader were being challenged to recognize his first impulse to laugh, get it over at the outset, and dismiss it for the rest of the poem'
(Danby p.40)

It is certainly true that Wordsworth has designs on the readers' sensibilities. It is also true that Wordsworth's tone changes in the poem. It is worth tracing these modulations of tone in a careful reading (e.g. in line 23).

The 'gratitude' of men (line 103) is one of the themes of the poem that could be expanded in discussion. Godwin (see **Cultural and Literary Background**) thought that gratitude should not be regarded as a virtue, because it was the sentiment the poor had to show to the rich when given something that should have been theirs by right.

> Gratitude is the product of inequality. Does Wordsworth challenge this view? What do the last two lines of the poem mean?

Anecdote for Fathers **and** We are Seven

It is useful to consider these two poems together. They both have a speaker describing an encounter with a child, a dialogue which ends in the child's view prevailing. Both are written in a simple, ballad-like form. It would be helpful to explore the differences also. In *We are Seven* the speaker is still convinced that there are only five left, while in *Anecdote for Fathers*, the speaker realizes his foolishness in repeatedly questioning a small child. Both poems works on the opposition between the rational adult mind and the intuitive sensations of the child.

Which is more successful as a poem?

Lines written in early Spring

Although written in a ballad-like stanza (the second line is longer than in the standard ballad), the poem is subjective and meditative. The harmony and almost sentient joy of Wordsworth's natural surroundings leads him to consider the human world. The contrast saddens him.

> Look at the victims described in this volume of poems to see 'what man has made of man'. Then look at what was happening in the decade before 1798. You could also look at the mood and atmosphere of *Lines written at a small distance* and compare them with this poem.

The Thorn

Many critics, following Wordsworth's own interest in him, have concentrated on the psychology of the narrator. They emphasize the centrality of his superstitious imagination and how this is shown at work in the story.

Another approach would concentrate on the actual story and look at the figure of Martha Ray. She connects up with other female victims in *Lyrical Ballads*. It would be useful to compare her with the figure of the Female Vagrant. Both are victims of society, but there is a great difference in the treatment of each woman.

A third approach would be by careful study of the natural imagery of the poem. Thorn, pond and mound have symbolic resonances.

The Last of the Flock

The poet describes an encounter with a member of the rural poor, first placing him powerfully as a uniquely pitiful sight – a healthy man crying on the road and carrying a lamb. He then allows the man to speak and the rest of the poem is an impassioned emotional outburst describing his condition. He has had to sell his flock to feed his family. The poem considers the idea of property. (The early stanzas of *The Female Vagrant* also describe a peaceful and prosperous time when the girl herded her flock.) Owning his flock has given the shepherd stability, happiness and a sense of self-worth. But what is his relationship to his children? Is there a hint of resentment in his obsessive passion?

Wordsworth is eliciting quite a complex response from the reader on the subject of the shepherd's loss.

> Compare the poem with *The Begger's Petition* published in *The Gentle-man's Magazine*, May 1791. (See **Appendix**, page 240.)

The Dungeon
Coleridge's radical Romantic views on prison reform can be connected not only with the preoccupations of the 1790s, but also with the central tenet of Romanticism – that the natural world is a healer and a teacher. The 'child of nature becomes in some sense the human ideal' (Holmes, 190). This is what Coleridge wants for his baby, Hartley, at the end of *The Nightingale* (and in *Frost at Midnight*, published later). This is also what the Mariner learns.

> Compare this poem with Wordworth's *The Convict*. Look at the form each poet has chosen. Which is more successful for this particular subject?

The Mad Mother
The subject matter, despite its anecdotal origins, is similar to that of the folk ballads in Percy's *Reliques* – a woman passionately addressing her child. Some critics have suggested that this poem and *The Complaint of a Forsaken Indian Woman* are coded expressions of guilt and remorse over Annette Vallon, the woman Wordsworth left pregnant in France. (Moorman notes similarities of vocabulary between Annette's letters and some of the stanzas in this poem.)

The woman's madness is conveyed through her obsessive and contra-dictory references to her husband and her simplistic fantasies of life 'underneath the spreading tree' (line 73) where she will live with her son on 'earth nuts' (line 96). Compare this with the realistic attitude of *The Female Vagrant*.

But Wordsworth shows the importance of the mother-child bond. It is the only thing that draws the woman back into some sort of sanity. The child saves the mother. At the time, it was thought that breast-feed-ing would alleviate post-natal depression (lines 31–32).

The 'fiendish faces' (line 23) that the woman recalls at her breast may refer to the practice of wet-nursing, where poor women who were lac-tating would earn money by suckling other women's babies, often to the detriment of their own child's health. Or the reference may be to night-mares.

The poem is not as simple as it appears. It certainly repays close reading. The monologue does not allow for authorial intervention or direction.

> Compare and contrast *The Mad Mother* with *The Female Vagrant* and *The Complaint of a Forsaken Indian Woman*. Explore Wordsworth's interest in the human mind on the edge and in extremity. What do people feel at this time and how are these emotions expressed?

The Idiot Boy
Wordsworth's attitude to 'Idiots' was revealed in a letter to John Wilson in 1802, when he was defending his choice of subject matter in *The Idiot Boy*:

'I have often applied to Idiots, in my own mind, that sublime expression of Scripture, that "their life is hidden with God". They are worshipped, probably from a feeling of this sort, in several parts of the East.

Among the Alps, where they are numerous, they are considered, I believe, as a blessing to the family to which they belong. I have indeed often looked upon the conduct of fathers and mothers of the lower classes of society towards Idiots as the great triumph of the human heart.'

This idea of the 'Idiot' as almost holy, a sacramental being who is the cause of heroic emotional conduct in others, is not shared by Coleridge in his critique of *The Idiot Boy*:

'Two following charges.....The one is, that the author has not, in the poem itself, taken sufficient care to preclude from the reader's fancy the disgusting images of ordinary morbid idiocy, which yet it was by no means his intention to represent. He has even by the "burr, burr, burr", uncounteracted by any preceding description of the boy's beauty, assisted in recalling them. The other is, the idiocy of the boy is so evenly balanced by the folly of the mother, as to present to the general reader rather a laughable burlesque on the blindness of anile dotage, than an analytic display of maternal affection in its ordinary workings'. (***Biographia Literaria***, 1817, ii 48–49).

1. For a long time critics agreed with Coleridge. However, for the last forty years, critics have been re-evaluating the poem, finding deliberate humour in the mock-solemn tone, the frettings of Betty, the spontaneous cure of Susan, the endless runnings around in the night. Others have stressed the complexities of the narrative, the varying emotions and tensions of Betty, or Wordsworth stressing the problems he has as a poet

with the subject matter. This is a complicated text which needs careful reading.

2. Betty's great love and care for her son should be put in the context of a society which was beginning to confine the mentally ill in workhouses and asylums. This was much more the case in the South of England and Wordsworth had been shocked by it. In the North, lunatics and 'idiots' were more likely to be free. *The Idiot Boy* is making a case for the mother to care for the 'idiot boy', not the institution. It is a debate with a great deal of contemporary resonance, now that the merits of 'care in the community' as against secure confinement are again under close scrutiny.

3. Contrasted with the three protagonists (five if the doctor and pony are counted) is the natural world itself. Critics have made a case for an affinity between the natural world and the 'Idiot Boy'. The boy has no rational logical mind to get in the way of his direct response to Nature. He will never grow away from this affinity with the natural world for he will never grow up. Even words do not get in his way. He does not know the words 'moon' and 'owl'. Is this why Wordsworth only 'guesses' what happens to him during the night? This is the part of the story he refuses to tell.

4. The boy can be seen as one of Wordsworth's outcasts, but a fortunate one whose simplicity is a kind of holy innocence and who is surrounded by love, even when, like the other less fortunate outcasts, he is separated from it.

Follow up these differing approaches:

Look very carefully at the poet's tone and show how he directs and orchestrates the action (for example his use of questions, lines 7–10; the use of the present tense; the progression of the clock; the dramatic pointers, line 257; the address to the reader, line 322; the series of references directing the reader's attention to the difficulties of writing the central experience of the poem, lines 232–56; by the series of 'perhaps' etc.)

The spontaneous cure of Susan should be closely scrutinized. Is she cured 'as if by magic' (line 436) or does she get better because of her affection and care for her neighbours?

Notice also Wordsworth's repetition of a particular phrase in the early part of the poem: 'Him whom she loves, her idiot boy'. This poem follows *The Mad Mother*, where the mad woman's love for her baby helps to stabilize her (sometimes). Is there a suggestion in this poem of the redemptive power of the mother's love? If so, who does it redeem, Betty or her son?

Find out about changing attitudes to the mentally handicapped in the late eighteenth century so that you can put this poem more thoroughly in its social context.

Follow up all references to the natural world. Show how it contrasts with the words, thoughts and actions of Betty, Susan and the Doctor. Can you find affinities between the boy and Nature?

Contrast *The Idiot Boy* with other 'outcast' poems in **Lyrical Ballads**, e.g. *The Thorn* or *Old Man Travelling*.

Lines written near Richmond, upon the Thames, at Evening

This poem was included in later editions of **Lyrical Ballads** but, on Coleridge's advice, it was printed as two poems, having been divided between the second and third stanzas. This certainly corresponds with what seems like a break in the poem.

One approach to this poem is by focusing on style, and by practical criticism; analyse some eighteenth century conventions (e.g. personification, periphrasis). Compare *Lines* lines 1 – 24 and *Tintern Abbey* lines 1 – 23.

Another approach is to look at the thematic content. There is the concern, characteristic of this volume, with the relation between the human and natural worlds. Paramount here is the effect that the natural scene has on the observer, conveying both the ephemeral quality of the experience and the enduring quality of the environment. There is the concern with the poet and his special 'visions'. Here Wordsworth connects the figure of the young poet with earlier poets he admired, perhaps placing himself among the hierarchy. But note that this is a hierarchy where feeling is seen as most important (lines 14 – 16, 35–6). In *The Leech Gatherer* (1802), he sees himself in relation to a line of 'mighty poets in their misery dead', in whose number he included Chatterton and Burns.

Expostulation and Reply and *The Tables Turned*

These are key poems in **Lyrical Ballads**. They are a statement of Wordsworth's convictions (of the late 1790s) and are cornerstones of a particular sort of Romanticism which was very influential in nineteenth-century England. The Victorians found these poems particularly congenial, perhaps because of their uplifting and 'philosophical' message.

Critics have noticed the oddity of choosing ballad-like quatrains to engage in a philosophical debate. A more suitable form, allowing for more flexible argument, would have been close to hand in the 'Conversation' blank verse form that Coleridge was developing and was using in *The Nightingale* during April 1798, and which Wordsworth used for *Tintern Abbey* in July 1798. It is worth looking again at *The Nightingale* after reading these two shorter pieces, because Coleridge is also asking his companions to come and listen to birdsong to discover a reality that literary types stuck indoors are misrepresenting.

Hazlitt, who was perhaps one of the models for 'Matthew' recalled:

'I got into a metaphysical argument with Wordsworth, while Coleridge was explaining the different notes of the nightingale to his sister, in which we neither of us succeeded in making ourselves perfectly clear and intelligible.'

(*My First Acquaintance with Poets*, 1823)

Wordsworth's statement in the Advertisement must recall the same incident. These two poems 'arose out of conversation with a friend who was somewhat unreasonably attached to modern books of moral philosophy'.

Again, this shows an oddness – this time of vocabulary. Wordsworth is objecting to his friend being 'unreasonable' while in the poem he attacks rationality. This is the same sort of paradox as choosing a ballad-like stanza to convey rather abstract philosophical thoughts.

Wordsworth is attacking rationality and analytical intellectual pursuits. He posits another sort of 'knowing'. This comes about through developing a relationship with the external universe.

The best way to approach these two poems is to address this central issue and see how it is the crucial focus of *Lyrical Ballads*.

> Explore the different ways Wordsworth and Coleridge approach this central meaning. What forms do they use? But start by specific examination. Look at particular issues in these two poems: for example
>
> 1 Look at the way the word 'light' is used in different ways (*Expostulation* line 5 and *Tables* line 15).
>
> 2 Examine the use of 'leaves' (*Tables* line 30).

3 Note the role of the senses in *Expostulation* lines 17–20.

4 Make a list of what 'Nature' or the 'powers' can do, e.g. 'impress' (look at the literal meaning of this); 'feed', 'teach', 'bless' etc.

5 What can man do to develop this relationship?

6 Look at the pivotal stanza in *Expostulation*. Can you see anything significant in lines 13–14?

Old Man Travelling

'Throughout 1797 debate had been carried on in Parliament, in books and in pamphlets, and in the correspondence columns of the magazines on how best to cope with the growing mass of the absolutely impoverished.' (Gill p.140)

Wordsworth's *The Old Cumberland Beggar* was part of this debate and *Old Man Travelling* (developed from the earlier poem) should be seen in this context. It should also be seen in the context of the war with France and the suffering that this caused ordinary people. Students could follow this approach by reading accounts of provision for the poor in the 1790s, especially concentrating on the 1797 'Bill for the better Support and Maintenance of the Poor' which caused a wide range of public response.

Another approach would be to look closely at the way Wordsworth describes the old man. There is a complexity here. His 'animal tranquillity' co-exists with 'thought'. He is a man, but the birds have no fear of him. Wordsworth was constantly drawn to the figure of the vagrant, who by long wandering and association with Nature, had taken on some of the characteristics of the natural world. These manifested themselves as moral virtues. His poem *The Old Leech Gatherer* (1802) is a good example of this. Students could follow this up, by finding out more about the philosopher Hartley and 'Associationism' (see **Cultural and Literary Background**, page 216).

The third approach would be to consider the juxtaposition of the natural 'decay' of the old man and the premature and shocking 'dying' of his son. Critics have felt that here, as in some other poems in *Lyrical Ballads*, Wordsworth intended to manipulate and de-familiarize the reader. Is Wordsworth manipulating the readers' emotions deliberately to shock? Are we too ready to accept the author's middle-class voice? The real experience conveyed by the voice of the poor old man questions that assumption. And if the reader is wrong to believe that middle-class voice who talks so confidently about the poor, then maybe the reader is wrong to believe other middle-class voices in poems, magazines and newspapers who talk so confidently about the poor.

Later, after 1805, Wordsworth changed the whole effect of the poem by suppressing lines 15–20. The title *Old Man Travelling* was discarded (1800) and the more abstract subtitle adopted. Was this a political cop-out? Or was he making a better poem?

The Complaint of a Forsaken Indian Woman

This poem should be seen in relation to *The Mad Mother*, *The Female Vagrant* etc., as another study of a woman, outcast and left to die in a natural world which does not seem on the surface to offer much relief. The Indian woman is separated from her natural kinship with her child and in stanza 3 she tries to convince herself of the child's surviving consciousness of the bond.

Whatever the reasons for the number of bereft female figures in *Lyrical Ballads* – whether it is due to Wordsworth's feelings of personal guilt, or his use of a conventional device, or both – it would be helpful to compare and contrast them all, looking particularly at:

1 Woman as social victim

2 Wordsworth's representation of the mother-child bond

3 Relationship between the isolated woman figure and the natural world.

The Convict

This poem, dropped from later editions of *Lyrical Ballads*, should be seen as an early piece written when Wordsworth was still influenced by Godwin, whose philosophy he later came to reject. Godwin's own interest in justice and the law can be seen in his extraordinarily gripping novel *Caleb Williams*, published in 1794, where he shows how the law works in the interests of the ruling classes. The treatment of prisoners is a theme returned to in *Lyrical Ballads* and should be seen in relation to the views of Wordsworth and Coleridge on the beneficial effects of the natural world.

Lines written a few miles above Tintern Abbey, on revisiting the banks of the Wye during a tour, July 13, 1798

Critics have always regarded this as a major poem. Contemporary critics welcomed it, having recognized its eighteenth-century roots. The Victorians saw it as a central therapeutic text.

1 Many twentieth-century critics have regarded it as a great poem of affirmation, celebrating the unity of Nature and humankind. One of them, M.H. Abrams, has called this type of poem 'the greater Romantic lyric' (Hilles and Bloom). Like Coleridge's 'Conversation' poems (from which Wordsworth derived a great deal), the 'greater Romantic lyric' is a meditation on a particular scene which leads to insight. Keats and Shelley both wrote this type of poem and, as a form, it has been very influential. It generally deals with significant issues and students can follow this line by looking at Wordsworth's preoccupations in this poem. They are:

a) the action of Memory; b) the process of Time; c) the nature of Loss; d) the struggle to rescue something for the future.

Look at the concept of 'unity' by examining the use of 'All' in the poem. It is used sixteen times.

'We' replaces 'I'. When does it happen and what does it represent?

2 More recent critics have found problems with the poem. How does it relate to the other poems in the volume – the poems of rural realism about deserted women, convicts, poverty-stricken old men?

Look at the outcasts – how do they relate to Wordsworth's resolutions and reconciliations (lines 89–94 and lines 103–12)?

3 Why does Wordsworth suddenly address his sister and assume that her future experiences will mirror his? Feminist critics have questioned his expectation that she will behave and grow in a particular way (lines 118–60).

Does Wordsworth 'disappear' from the poem when he addresses his sister? Does he hand everything over to her? What do you think?

4 It has also been said that the poem's specific dating in the sub-title – July 13 1798 – must draw attention to its historical context. July 13th is the eve of Bastille Day, one of the most significant early dates in the French Revolution. When Wordsworth talks about 'five years' he implies as well as rejects the events of the 1790s – the course of the French Revolution, the war with France, the worsening plight of the poor. Between 1797 and 1798, there was an Irish rebellion, an invasion threat, the

first execution for treason in England. This is the immediate context for *Tintern Abbey*.

Some critics have pointed out that disturbing elements – not only in contemporary politics, but also in the scene he describes himself as observing (the abbey, a ruin overrun by beggars) – are edited out by the poet (Campbell). Is this important? Do you feel that Wordsworth is deflecting and displacing social realities so that he can assert his personal vision?

Essays

1 What effect does Coleridge achieve by the contrast of the 'frame' wedding story and the story of the Mariner?

2 Does the experience of the Mariner bear out the 'moral' – 'he prayeth best who loveth best'? Are you convinced? State your reasons.

3 The 1817 version of *The Rime of the Ancient Mariner* has a 'gloss' which states and explains the moral themes to the reader. Find a copy of the poem with Coleridge's gloss and read it carefully. Which version do you prefer? Why?

4 Discuss the use of Christian imagery in *The Rime of the Ancyent Marinere*. Is this disrupted at any point? What effects does Coleridge achieve by this imagery?

5 Compare Wordsworth's *Lines left upon a Seat in a Yew-tree* with *Tintern Abbey*, paying particular attention to Wordsworth's ideas about man and nature.

6 Discuss Wordsworth's representations of women in *The Thorn* and *The Female Vagrant*. Compare these with *The Prostitute* (Appendix).

7 Show how Wordsworth's dramatic representation of the shepherd in *The Last of the Flock* works by comparing it with *The Beggar's Petition* (Appendix).

8 'Have I not reason to lament
  What man has made of man?'

What *has* man made of man, judging by the evidence of *Lyrical Ballads*? Discuss by referring to three poems in detail but mention more.

9 Show Wordsworth's attempts to understand the workings of the human mind by examining *Tintern Abbey*.

10 Discuss the possibilities and limitations of the ballad form and blank verse by comparing and contrasting two poems.

11 Compare the diction of four poems in *Lyrical Ballads* and show how effective each is (e.g. *The Nightingale* – conversation; *Lines left upon a Seat in a Yew-tree* – elevated; *The Idiot Boy* – colloquial; *The Rime of the Ancyent Marinere* – archaic).

12 Many of the characters in *Lyrical Ballads* are miserable, outcast, isolated. Why? Is it their fault? Is it the fault of society? Is it to do simply with the condition of being human? Do Wordsworth or Coleridge make any moral judgements on these outcasts?

13 Discuss the attitudes of Wordsworth and Coleridge towards the criminal. Are they similar? How do they represent the criminal? Compare with the attitudes expressed in *The Prison* and *On the Necessity of Solitary Confinement in Gaols* (Appendix).

14 In 1798 *Lyrical Ballads* was published anonymously. It was read as a text written by one author. What connections can you find between *The Rime of the Ancyent Marinere* and *Tintern Abbey* which make this feasible?

15 Look at the ordering of the poems in *Lyrical Ballads*. In later editions Wordsworth changed the order (for example, he put *Rime of the Ancyent Marinere* at the end). Can you find thematic connections or contrasts which make this particular sequence a reasonable arrangement?

16 Making reference to two poems, explore the relationships between man and nature that Wordsworth and Coleridge describe. Compare and contrast the two.

WRITING AN ESSAY
ABOUT POETRY

Your own personal response to a poet and his or her work is of major importance when writing an essay on poetry, either as part of your course or as an examination question. However, this personal response needs to be based on a solid concept of how poetry works, so you must clearly show that you understand the methods the poet uses to convey the message and ideas of the poem to the reader. In most cases, unless it is relevant to your answer, you should not pad out your essay with biographical or background material.

Planning

Look carefully at the wording of the question. Underline the important words and ideas. Make sure you apply your mind to these key elements of the question and then explore them in the essay.

Bring all your knowledge of, and opinions on, a poet and his or her poetry to this first stage of writing. Brainstorm your ideas and always combine these thoughts in a plan that shows the development and intention of your answer. Your plan must outline the structure of your essay. In exam conditions, the plan and the direction of your comments may take you only a few minutes and should be little more than a way of laying out your ideas in order. However the plan must be an outline of how and where you are going to link your evidence to the opinions and concepts of the essay. Reject any ideas which are not relevant at the planning stage. Remember that your plan should be arranged around your ideas and not the chronological order of a poem or a poet's work, or your essay will be weakened.

Writing

Your introduction must implicitly or, if you wish, explicitly make the teacher or examiner realize that you understand the question.

Don't spend a lot of time spotting, defining and examining poetic techniques and form. If you do identify these features, then you must be sure of the poetic terms and be able to show why they are significant in the verse and to the poet's attempts to create a 'meaning' and a message.

Make absolutely sure that your answer is clear and that it tackles the issues in the question precisely. Try to offer points for discussion and apply your knowledge in an interesting way. Don't go ahead and disregard what the question asks you to write about, then write the essay you want to write. Don't waffle, don't write too elaborately or use terms vaguely; at the same time, don't be too heavy-handed with your views. Strive to put your opinions directly and accurately.

In exam conditions be aware of the time, and if you are running out of your allotted span then make sure that you put down your most important ideas in the minutes left. Try to leave a few minutes to revise and proof-read your script. Be sure that the points you have made make sense and are well supported by evidence. Don't try to introduce new ideas as you write unless they are essential to your essay. Often these extra thoughts can distract you from the logic of your argument. If it is essential, then refer back to your plan and slot the idea into the right part of the essay.

Bring your ideas together at the end of the essay. Make sure that you have put your views clearly and, if necessary, express the main thrust of your views or argument again.

Quotations

Quotations are a vital source of evidence for the viewpoints and ideas you express in your essay. Try not to misquote and remember that when using extracts of more than a few words you should place them separately outside your text as they would be laid out in the poem.

If you follow the advice here you will produce a clear, relevant and logical essay. Try to spend time reading and listening to the comments of your teacher and make your own notes on your work for revision purposes.

A NOTE FROM A CHIEF EXAMINER

Your examination script is the medium through which you communicate with your examiner. As a student, you will have studied what writers say and how they say it; your examiner will assess what *you* say and how you say it. This is the simple process through which your knowledge and understanding of the texts you have studied is converted into your examination result.

The questions which you will find on your examination paper have been designed to enable you to display your ability to engage in short, highly concentrated explorations of particular aspects of the texts which you have studied. There is no intention to trick you into making mistakes, rather to enable you to demonstrate to your examiner your knowledge and understanding. Questions take a variety of forms. For a poetry text, you may be asked to concentrate on one poem, or a particular group of them, and provide detailed examination of some features of the writing. You may be asked to range widely throughout a poet's work, exploring specified aspects of his or her style and themes. You may be asked to provide a considered personal reaction to a critical evaluation of the poet's work.

Whatever the question, you are, ultimately, being asked to explore what and how, content and style. Equally, you are being asked for a personal response. You are communicating to your examiner your own understanding of the text, and your reactions to it, based on the studies you have undertaken.

All of this may seem very simple, if not self-evident, but it is worthwhile to devote some time to thinking about what an examination is, and how it works. By doing so, you will understand why it is so important that you should prepare yourself for your examination in two principal ways: first, by thorough, thoughtful and analytical textual study, making your own well-informed evaluation of the work of a particular writer, considering what he or she is conveying to you, how this is done, how you react, and what has made you respond in that way; then, by practising the writing skills which you will need to convey all these things to your examiner.

When assessing your script and awarding marks, examiners are working to guidelines which instruct them to look for a variety of different qualities in an essay.

These are some of the things which an examiner will consider.

- How well has the candidate understood the essay question and the given task? Is the argument, and the material used to support it, entirely relevant?

- Is quotation used aptly, and textual reference employed skilfully in discussion?

- Is the candidate aware of how and why the writer has crafted material in a particular way?

- Is there evidence of engagement with the text, close analytical reading, and awareness of subtleties in interpretation?

- Does the candidate have the necessary vocabulary, both general and critical, to express his or her understanding lucidly? Are technical terms integrated into discussion?

- Can the candidate provide an interesting, clearly expressed and structured line of argument, which fully displays a well-informed personal response?

From these points, you should be able to see the kind of approach to examination questions which you should avoid. Re-hashed notes, second-hand opinion, unsupported assertion and arid copies of marginal jottings have no place in a good script. Don't fall into the trap of reproducing a pre-planned essay. Undoubtedly you will find (if your preparation has been thorough) that you are drawing on ideas which you have already explored in other essays, but all material used must be properly adapted to the task you are given. Don't take a narrative approach; paraphrase cannot replace analysis. Do not, under any circumstances, copy out chunks of introduction or critical notes from your text in an open book examination. Nor do you need to quote at excessive length; your examiner knows the text.

It is inevitable that, when writing in examination conditions, you will only use quite a small amount of the material you have studied in order to answer a particular question. Don't feel that what you are not using has been wasted. It hasn't. All your studies will have informed the understanding you display in a succinct, well-focused answer, and will equip you to write a good essay.

Virginia Graham

APPENDIX

The Beggar's Petition

Pity the sorrows of a poor old man,
Whose trembling limbs have born him to your door;
Whose days are dwindled to the shortest span: –
Oh, give relief and Heav'n will bless your store.

5   These tatter'd cloaths my poverty bespeak;
These hoary locks proclaim my lengthened years;
And many a furrow in my grief-worn cheek
Has been the channel to a flood of tears!

Yon house, erected on the rising ground,
10 With tempting aspect, drew me from my road;
For Plenty there a residence has found,
And Grandeur a magnificent abode.

Hard is the fate of the infirm and poor!
Here, as I crav'd a morsel of their bread,
15 A pampered menial drove me from the door,
To seek a shelter in a humbler shed.

Oh, take me to your hospitable dome!
Keen blows the wind and piercing is the cold!
Short is my passage to the friendly tomb;
20 For I am poor and miserably old!

Should I reveal the sources of my grief,
If soft Humanity e'er touched your breast,
Your hands would not withhold the kind relief,
And tears of Pity would not be represt.

25 Heav'n sends misfortunes! Why should we repine? –
'Tis Heav'n has brought me to the state you see! –
And your condition soon may be like mine,
The child of Sorrow and of Misery!

A little farm was my paternal lot;
30 Then, like the lark, I sprightly hail'd the morn!
But, ah! Oppression forced me from my cot;
My cattle died, and blighted was my corn.

My daughter, once the comfort of my age,
Lur'd by a villain from her native home,
35 Is cast, abandon'd, on the world's wide stage,
And doomed in scanty poverty to roam.

My tender wife, sweet soother of my cares,
Struck with sad anguish at the stern decree;
Fell, ling'ring, fell, a victim of Despair,
40 And left the world to wretchedness and me!

Pity the sorrows of a poor old man,
Whose trembling limbs have borne him to your door;
Whose days are dwindled to the shortest span;
Oh, give relief, and Heav'n will bless your store!
                    (*The Gentleman's Magazine*, September 1791.)

Extract from
On the Necessity of Solitary Confinement in Gaols

'It is doing little to restrain the bad by punishments, unless you render
them good by discipline.' (Inscription on a house of correction at Rome)

See, in the place where vice should meet a cure,
A wretched herd, with hearts and hands impure
Formed in a band to fit for greater harms
The young offender – fled from Virtue's charms.
5 Here he is taught to laugh at weeping friends,
And gracious counsel which their pity sends:
A partner's sorrows, with her infant train,
Beg for admission to his heart in vain:
Or, if he listens to their tender plaint,
10 And cheer the heart, by grief and sickness faint –

Points their last hope to scenes of future joy,
When he, releas'd, will all his powers employ
In the fond charge of Father, Husband, Friend,
And with his life his future kindness end: –
15 Alas! his vows and promises are vain,
He but returns to that black band again,
And all is lost! – a Father's tender care,
A Husband's pity – all is buried there
In pois'nous converse! and, at length, unchain'd
20 (His more than savage passions unrestrain'd)
He falls a victim to that fatal plan,
Fatal to Virtue, and to feeble man.

(by 'Achates', *The Gentleman's Magazine*, March 1792)

The Prostitute

Poor profligate! I will not chide thy sins,
What, though the coldly virtuous turn away,
And the proud priest shall stalk indignant by,
And deem himself polluted, should he hold
5   A moment's converse with thy guilty soul.
Yet thou shall have my tear, to such as thou
Sinful, abas'd and unbefriended, came
The World's great Saviour; from his gentle lip
No word of high reproof or bitter scorn
10 Fell chilly; but his exhortation mild
Bade the meek radiance of celestial hope
Beam on the faded brow "Who first shall throw
Against this women the accusing stone?"
Sullen behold the envious Levite shrink,
15 Whispering his mutter'd curse of angry shame,
Whilst busy conscience slumbers now no more.
Hear this, ye hard reprovers of mankind,
Ye, to the charms of taste and fancy dead,
Who through the world's tumultuous passage keep
20 Your cold and even tenor; hear and blush,
Ye unkind comforters, who, as ye pour

The nauseous poison of the keen reproof
In Pharasaic spleen, are studious more
To boast the virtues of your own proud hearts
25 Than medicine with hope the trembling wretch
That calls on you to bless his parting breath.
Yes, hapless outcast, thou shalt have my tear;
Thou once wast fairer than the morning-light,
Thy breast unsullied as the meadow's flower
30 Wash'd by the dews of May – What, if thine eye,
Once eloquent to speak the souls's pure thought,
Dart with insidious leer the lustful glance;
What, if thy breast, which in thy morn of life,
Just kindling to the infant thought of love,
35 Trembled in sweet confusion, rudely now
Pant with fierce passion, and more fierce despair;
What if thine alter'd voice, no longer soft
Or plaintive, hoarsely meet the startled ear
With horrid imprecation – Not on thee
40 Shall fall the curse of Heaven, but on the wretch,
Fell as the lion on Numidia's wilds,
That, with blood-streaming fangs and bristling mane
Growls o'er his human banquet – on the wretch,
Who, dress'd in sunny smiles and April tears,
50 Won on thy virgin heart, and, having cropt,
Briefly, the luscious flesh of thy young love,
Soon left thee as the poor and naked stalk,
Now worthless; to abide the wintry blast,
The chilling tempest of the world's proud scorn,
55 Say, when with fault'ring tongue and downcast eye,
He spake delicious musick, and thine heart
Suspected not deceit; and as he press'd
Thy throbbing bosom to his burning lips;
O'er all thy frame the soft delirium stole;
60 Oh! could thy cheated fancy dare to think
That one so dear to thy deluded heart,
So prodigal of vows, could coldly turn
And smile at thy undoing, as the theme
Of youthful triumph! Yes, he left thee thus
65 Thy parents' curse, the world's unpity'd scorn,

To earn the fleeting wages of disgrace,
Thy sad remains of life to linger out
In hopeless prostitution. Dead to shame
And penitence, which all would now refuse
70 And shun thee as the pestilential blight;
No hope awaits thee, but in Him alone
Who knows each secret spring that moves the heart,
And with no narrow justice rules the world.
Farewell, poor profligate! and as I give
75 The trifle to avert tomorrow's want,
Should no licentious drunkard make thee rich,
Oh! could I to thy bosom's hell impart
One ray of that pure light of virtuous thought,
Which, ere the foul seducer ravening came
80 Glow'd with mild lustre in thine angel-face!
          (by Thomas Lister Esq., *The Gentleman's Magazine*, July 1798)

A Prison

Here pines the wretch to each fine feeling dead,
His breast with woe and sadness torn;
On his hard couch he lays his heavy head,
Unmourned, unpity'd, and forlorn.

5   The sun-beams cast a melancholy ray,
The grates admit but little air,
The gloomy light just shews the hapless prey
Of hope deferr'd and wild despair.

When sinking feeble on the humid ground,
10   What grief, what anguish wrings his heart;
He faintly turns his languid eyes around,
Pierc'd by Affliction's pois'nous dart.

His dry-parch'd lips evince continual thirst,
The voice of joy ne'er meets his ear.
15   His briny tears now moisten his stale crust;
His mind contending passions tear.

Strange unknown fears possess his anxious breast,
When midnight spreads her darksome gloom;
His harass'd spirits want their nat'ral rest,
20 When frightful objects fill the room.

Gigantic figures stalk with silent head,
Which Superstition wildly rears;
He starts convulsive from his hard-worn bed,
His weary bosom Madness tears.

25 Heart rending Woe here to herself bemoans,
And sheds a sad and daily tear;
The vaulted roof re-echoes to her groans
No friendly eye, no succour near.

(By 'Cinna', *The Gentleman's Magazine*, September 1798)

The Beggar-Boy

When blows the cold and piercing wind,
And Nature's drest in robes of snow,
And you, with friends so free and kind,
Of Winter's blasts do little know;
5 In dance and song your hours enjoy
Nor heed the tempest's roar;
Ah! think on the poor Beggar-boy
That's shiv'ring at your door!

His parents once like you were gay,
10 Like you enjoy'd their revelry;
But intercepted was that ray
Of mirth by clouds of penury.
By dire disease, to want brought nigh,
Their hearts could bear no more,
15 They died! and left the Beggar-boy
That's shiv'ring at your door!

Say, have you known a father's love?
Or felt a mother's fost'ring care?
You have! – O then let pity move
20 Your hearts to once a darling rare!
The father's life – the mother's joy –
Than him was none lov'd more,
Than him, who now a Beggar-boy,
Stands shiv'ring at your door!

25 O! spare from your luxurious board
A morsel small for his relief;
A cast-off garment too afford,
And kindly heal the wounds of grief.
Then ev'ry blessing man enjoy
30 May you have o'er and o'er!
So hopes, so prays, the Beggar-Boy
That's shiv'ring at your door.

(*The Gentleman's Magazine*, September 1798)

SELECT BIBLIOGRAPHY

Further reading

Campbell, Patrick, *Wordsworth and Coleridge Lyrical Ballads*. 1991. Macmillan Critical Perspectives. London: Macmillan
A lively and informative discussion of the collection, which has proved invaluable in compiling this edition.

Brett, R.L. and Jones, A.R. (eds), *Wordsworth and Coleridge Lyrical Ballads* (second edition). 1991. London: Routledge.
A very useful text which includes 1800 and 1802 editions.

Darbishire, Helen (ed.) *Journals of Dorothy Wordsworth*. 1958. Oxford: The World's Classics.
This is invaluable when reading William Wordsworth or Coleridge. There are several editions of Dorothy's *Journals*, but some texts do not contain the Alfoxden Journal of 1798 which is necessary when studying *Lyrical Ballads*.

Matlak, Richard E. (ed.) *Approaches to Teaching Coleridge's Poetry and Prose*. 1991. New York: Modern Language Association of America.
This is particularly useful on approaching *The Ancyent Marinere*.

Lowes, John Livingston, *The Road to Xanadu*. 1927. Boston: Houghton Miflin Co.
A brilliant exploration of the genesis of *The Ancient Mariner* (and *Kubla Khan*) in Coleridge's reading and imagination.

Hall, Spencer with Ramsay, Jonathon, *Approaches to Teaching Wordsworth's Poetry*. 1986. New York: Modern Languages Association of America.
This is a very useful introduction to the problems of teaching *Lyrical Ballads*.

Homes, Richard, *Coleridge: Early Visions*. 1989. London: Hodder and Stoughton.
This volume of biography is a brilliant and uncensorious exploration of Coleridge as poet and thinker.

Gill, Stephen, *William Wordsworth: A Life*. 1989. Oxford: Clarendon Press.
A meticulous and sympathetic biography.

Glen, Heather, *Vision and Disenchantment: Blake's Songs and Wordsworth's*

Lyrical Ballads. 1983. Cambridge: Cambridge University Press.

A very interesting account of the work in relation to contemporary magazine poetry, contrasting the complexity of Wordsworth's poems with the moral banality of the magazines.

Hilles, F.W. and Bloom, H. (eds), *From Sensibility to Romanticism.* 1965. New York: Oxford University Press.

This contains the classic account of the 'greater Romantic lyric' (Abrams).

Butler, Marilyn, *Romantics, Rebels and Reactionaries.* 1981. Oxford: Oxford University Press.

A good contextual reading.

Also

Gravil, Richard, *Lyrical Ballads* (1798); Wordsworth as Ironist. *Critical Quarterly, XXIV,* no. 4.

Danby, John F., *The Simple Wordsworth.* 1960. London: Hodder and Stoughton.

Moorman, Mary, *William Wordsworth: A Biography. I The Early Years 1770–1803.* 1957. London: Oxford University Press.

Prickett, Stephen, *Wordsworth and Coleridge: The Lyrical Ballads.* 1975. London: Edward Arnold.

Coburn, Kathleen (ed.), *Coleridge, Twentieth-Century Views.* 1967. Englewood Cliffs, N.J.: Prentice Hall.

Jacobus, Mary, *Tradition and Experiment in Wordsworth's Lyrical Ballads 1798.* 1976. London: Oxford University Press.

Roe, Nicholas, *Wordsworth and Coleridge: the Radical Years.* 1988. Oxford: Clarendon Press.

Useful background reading

Newman, G., The Rise of English Nationalism: A Cultural History 1740–1830. 1987.

Rule, J., Albion's People: English Society 1714–1815. 1992.

Rude, G., Revolutionary Europe 1783–1815. 1964.

Schama, S., Citizens. 1989.

Harvey, A.D., English Poetry in a Changing Society, 1780–1825. 1980.

Purkis, J. The World of the English Romantic Poets. 1982.

Deane, P., The First Industrial Revolution. 1965.

Thompson, E.P., The Making of the English Working Class. 1963.

Laver, J., The Age of Illusion: Manners and Morals 1780–1850. 1976.

Trevelyan, G.M., English Social History. 1942.

Butler, M., Burke, Paine, Godwin and the Revolution Controversy. 1984.

Woodcock, B. and Coates, J., Combative Styles. Romantic Writing and Ideology: Two Contrasting Interpretations. 1994.

INDEX OF FIRST LINES